GREAT
REVIVALISTS

GREAT REVIVALISTS

1700 to the present day

JOHN PETERS

CWR

Published 2008 by CWR, Waverley Abbey House, Waverley Lane, Farnham, Surrey GU9 8EP, UK. Registered Charity No. 294387. Registered Limited Company No. 1990308.

Concept development, editing, design and production by CWR

Aimee Semple McPherson picture used by permission of the Heritage Department of the International Church of the Foursquare Gospel.

Printed in Croatia by Zrinski

ISBN: 978-1-85345-482-0

CONTENTS

A Survey of Revival 7

Timeline 28

David Brainerd 31

Duncan Campbell 35

Jonathan Edwards 39

Christmas Evans 43

Charles Grandison Finney 47

Howell Harris 51

Rees Howells 55

John 'Praying' Hyde 59

George Jeffreys 63

Stephen Jeffreys 67

John Kilpatrick 71

Dr Martyn Lloyd-Jones 75

David Morgan & Humphrey Jones 79

Robert Murray McCheyne 83

John Newton 87

Jessie Penn-Lewis 91

Evan Roberts 95

Aimee Semple McPherson 99

Charles Haddon Spurgeon 103

Charles Wesley 107

John Wesley 111

Susanna Wesley 115

George Whitefield 119

Smith Wigglesworth 123

David Yonggi Cho 127

Some Reflections: The Golden Threads 131

Conclusion 133

Select Bibliography 139

Charles Wesley

Jessie Penn-Lewis

Duncan Campbell

Rees Howells

John Newton

David Brainerd

John Wesley

George Whitefield

Susanna Wesley

Dr Martyn Lloyd-Jones

Charles Spurgeon

Charles Finney

Smith Wigglesworth

David Yonggi Cho

Aimee Semple McPherson

A SURVEY OF REVIVAL

Waverley Abbey House …
'a powerhouse for Jesus Christ'

This volume celebrates the twenty-first anniversary of Waverley Abbey House as the headquarters of CWR's operations throughout the world. Its acquisition came about after a reader of *Every Day with Jesus* contacted Selwyn Hughes (in 1982) suggesting that he should look at an old house which had recently become available for purchase. After receiving a second letter from the same correspondent, Selwyn and Trevor Partridge inspected the property which, at that time, was already on offer to another prospective buyer.

That was not, however, the end of the story. Eventually CWR's offer of £325,000 – not the highest by any means – was accepted. A protracted and complicated period of extensive renovation followed, with many significant technical and financial problems along the way, but on 29 August 1987, Lord Tonypandy (formerly Speaker of the House of Commons and possibly better known as George Thomas) conducted the opening ceremony. Selwyn spoke of the occasion as a milestone in the history of CWR and, for him, 'an exciting and emotional event'. Lord Tonypandy's words were prophetic: 'This place will be a powerhouse for Jesus Christ in the unfolding years … It will be used to train tomorrow's leaders in the Christian world.'

Since that auspicious occasion, Waverley Abbey House has been the ministry centre of CWR's global mission, been the location for many of its courses, housed the offices of its leaders and staff, and also witnessed a number of thrilling events. One such occasion was in 2002 on the fifteenth anniversary of the opening, when 1,000 people assembled in Waverley. Several speakers drew attention to the fact that the hallmark of Waverley is changed lives, with many of those who trained there having, quite literally, taken the teaching to help others around the world. Samson Gandhi, Executive Director of the Person to Person Counselling ministry in India at that time, commented that 'three weeks at Waverley in August 1996 redefined my personality, made me more like Christ, and set the path for my [whole] ministry. It was like a confirmation and commissioning.' Other speakers described how the courses at Waverley and the accompanying fellowship had provided the biblical foundations for their lives and work. In other words, God has used Waverley Abbey House to equip His people and His Church.

Other memorable events that spring to mind include Selwyn's address celebrating forty years of CWR and, perhaps most poignantly of all, his final address to CWR Partners and Staff in December 2005, just a few weeks before his death. Those present were impressed with his deeply held faith, conviction and courage; and his integrity left an indelible impression on everyone, together with a feeling that this was the end of a chapter and the beginning of a new era, as indeed it was.

In every sense, therefore, Waverley Abbey House is fulfilling the vision so bravely followed, in the first instance, by Selwyn and Trevor; it is appropriate that the 'coming of age' of the House should be marked and celebrated. The idea of a publication inevitably followed, but on which subject? The answer to such a query was, in many senses, obvious: revival and revivalists, the grassroots of CWR since its inception in 1965. Revival was, of course, one of the golden and sustaining threads of Selwyn Hughes' whole life, so no subject could be more apt.

Throughout his long ministry, Selwyn was careful to distinguish between renewal and revival; he often pondered on the reasons why some churches and commentators never moved beyond the idea of renewal to the more comprehensive idea of revival. In his editorial to the July/August 1988 issue of *Revival World Report* he said this:

> I am not sure I know the complete answer but my considered opinion is that it has to do with two things: one, our human tendency to be more preoccupied with getting a blessing than being a blessing, and two, a reluctance in allowing the Holy Spirit to clean up our lives. There is something in us all that settles for an experience of God rather than an encounter with God.

He added, with total justification, 'Any spiritual blessing that does not clean up our lives and deepen our prayer lives must be regarded as suspect.' Hard-hitting but true, and it was an emphasis he frequently returned to in his preaching, counselling and writing, in which he highlighted the danger of focusing on the spectacular phenomena and outwardly dramatic at the expense of losing our focus on the Lord Jesus. He certainly concurred with the views of Frank Bartleman, of Azusa Street fame, who said: 'We may not even hold a doctrine, or seek an experience, except in Christ. The attention of the people must be first of all, and always, held to him' (*Renewal*, 1995).

The nature of revival

'Revival is God bending down to the dying embers of a fire that is just about to go out, and breathing into it, until it bursts again into flame.' (Christmas Evans)
'A revival is something that can only be explained as the direct action and intervention of God.' (Dr Martyn Lloyd-Jones)
'Revival is something above and beyond that spiritual environment and climate which we, for want of a better word, deem normal.' (Vernon Higham)
'In revival, God visits His people, making His presence known and revealing Himself as the holy God. In revival people are overcome and overwhelmed by God's love.' (Robert Backhouse)

Two complementary truths are observable in all revivals. First, God's sovereignty. By sovereignty is meant God's absolute authority, thus meaning that revival (or 'times of refreshing') is always the action of God, not human beings. While it is true that the decisions of men and women can *end* revivals, they cannot *initiate* revival. To put the matter another way, revival is a movement of the Holy Spirit, a pouring out, if you wish, of His life and power. Aspects of this sovereignty, which often demonstrates itself when the Church is spiritually low, include:

+ fresh evidence of life-transforming Holy Spirit activity;
+ moral and ethical changes in society, as were abundantly evident in the 1904–05 revival in Wales;

9

- unusual or exceptional events causing the ongoing or normal activity of the Church to advance with extraordinary power;
- an emphasis on the holiness of God;
- a restoration of life in and to the Church in general and then, subsequently, to the world at large.

So revival is:

1. Seasonal, not perennial, because all revivals in history, by definition, have ended.
2. An action by God, something distinctly different in essence from spiritual conferences, however expertly organised and however gifted the preaching.
3. First to the Church, then it has its outworking in society and the world.
4. Characterised by an intense sense of God's presence.
5. Refreshing, but frequently results in controversy, as is clearly apparent in the experience of the Early Church (Acts 3:19).

'Those whom God uses in leadership in revival are always men who have met with God in a powerfully personal way and have a burning passion for the glory of God and a life of holiness. It is not possible for the Holy Spirit to come in great power upon his people without creating a longing for right and pure living.' (Brian Edwards)

The second complementary truth of revival relates to the work, influence and actions of men and women, or as Evan Roberts once famously said, in 1906, 'He is waiting for instruments.' By this he meant, of course, that God was – and is – looking for those people who will carry out His work, because revival is only possible, in one sense, through the human agency of men and women. God's choice in this respect is as sovereign and as authoritative as is His initiation of revival. So leaders of revival are chosen by God, and are His instruments to achieve His will and purpose.

Even a cursory glance at revival history shows that humility and prayerfulness are of pre-eminent importance, not gifting, either in terms of personality or intellect. The Welsh Revival 1904–05 provides an eloquent example and illustration of this principle. It was led by Evan Roberts who, in purely worldly terms, was considered by many to be a 'nonentity'. Inadequately educated, shy and retiring by nature, he was not a persuasive or fluent preacher, but it was he, rather than the more extravagantly gifted Peter Price, who was chosen to lead a movement with worldwide ramifications and which, to this day, stands as a 'classic' illustration of true revival. Price, admittedly, was better educated (a graduate of the University of Cambridge) and possessed of a more robust and dominating personality, but – and this is crucial – he was *not God's chosen instrument for Wales* at the start of the twentieth century. Fulminate though Price did with extravagant claims about the 'superiority of his revival in Dowlais', the principle of divine choice was unalterable and irrevocable: Roberts was born for such a time as that.

There were, in addition, key differences between Price and Roberts in several important areas. Roberts had built into his life qualities of integrity, character and faith that God could use in order to accomplish His (sovereign) purposes. What were they? He was disciplined and committed to the tasks given him, including the time when he worked underground in the mines; his fellow miners, well known for their robust, uncompromising criticism of anything pretentious, bogus or hypocritical, were high in their praise of the way he got on with the jobs allocated to him. He was serious-minded, open to the advice and direction of those in spiritual authority over him, while his own individual spiritual experience was intense and, often, all-consuming. He was devoted to prayer, and it was not unusual for him to pray throughout the night as he pleaded and agonised with God (for at least a decade before 1904) to pour out His Spirit on Wales. Over 100 years on from the revival, in which 'a heavenly nearness to God' was apparent, his own prayer for revival resonates with an almost unbearable intensity and sense of conviction, and is worth reproducing in full:

Lord Jesus, help us now through the Holy Spirit to come face to face with the Cross. Whatever the hindrance may be, we commit the service to Thee. Put us all under the Blood. Oh, Lord, place the Blood on all our past up to this moment. We thank Thee for the Blood.
Reveal the Cross through the Name of Jesus. Oh, open the Heavens. Descend upon us now. Tear open our hearts; give us such a sight of Calvary that our hearts may be broken. Oh Lord, descend now; open our hearts to receive the

heart that bled for us. If we are to be fools – make us fools for Thee. Take us,
spirit, soul, and body. WE ARE THINE. Thou hast purchased us.
Reveal the Cross for the sake of Jesus – the Cross that is to conquer the world.
Place us under the Blood. Forbid that we should think of what men may say
of us. Oh speak – speak – speak, Lord Jesus. Thy Words are 'wine indeed'.
Oh, reveal the Cross, beloved Jesus – the Cross in its glory.
Reign in every heart for the sake of Jesus. Lord, do Thou help us to see the
dying Saviour. Enable us to see Him conquering the hosts of darkness. Claim
victory for Thy Son, now Lord. He is worthy to have the victory. THOU ART
THE ALL-POWERFUL GOD. OH, CLAIM VICTORY. We shall give all the
glory to Thy Name. No one else has the right to the glory but Thee. Take it,
Lord. Glorify Thy Son in this meeting. OH, HOLY SPIRIT – DO THY WORK
THROUGH US AND IN US NOW. Speak Thy Word in power for Thy Name's
sake. Amen – and Amen!

Revival and the Bible

It is axiomatic that prayer is important both before and during revival. Equally relevant is the role of Scripture in revival. In general terms, reading the Bible is a vital part of the lives of Christians. In it, God speaks to us directly and personally, giving guidance (Psa. 119:105) and encouragement. The Bible is the source of our wisdom and the example of Paul is instructive: '… he reasoned with them [the Thessalonians] from the Scriptures' (Acts 17:2).

Knowledge of, and obedience to, the Bible is permanently enshrined in the history of revival, beginning in the Acts of the Apostles and continuing to the present day. Obedience to the Word of God is apparent in the lives of those who have led revivals, accepting its authority as a starting point and striving to obey it as guided by the Holy Spirit. It is not exaggeration to claim that God will not trust revival to any person who does rely explicitly on the teaching of the Bible. St Augustine's life of sensuality and carnal indulgence was transformed as he read Paul's epistle to the Romans, and the same book had an equally transforming effect on Martin Luther, both men significant leaders of revival. To these august figures might be added the names of Peter Waldo (twelfth century) John Wycliffe (fourteenth century), Jonathan Edwards (eighteenth century) and David (formerly Paul) Yonggi Cho (twentieth century).

Revival is supernatural. Through the Holy Spirit's dynamic influence the Church is restored so that it becomes the visible and dramatic demonstration of God's life and power. But it is not possible without reformation by His Word as an ongoing process. As Vernon Higham rightly says, '[In revival] people really come to know their Bibles and, when they pray, a wealth of scriptural passages and verses weave through their prayers. The revival of scriptural knowledge would also mean its application in people's lives.' Higham's emphasis accords entirely with the view of Charles Haddon Spurgeon's words: 'The Bible was not meant to increase our knowledge but to change our lives.' This is true whether we live in times of revival or not.

A most interesting suggestion regarding the link between prayer and Bible reading is found in T.M. Moore's book, *Preparing Your Church For Revival*. His overall thesis is that men and women who wait on God for revival and a fresh visitation of the Holy Spirit need to have a clear understanding of God's promises, be devoted to the ongoing work of the gospel, and follow biblical guidelines for their prayers. He says,

> The great advantage in using God's own words in our prayers for revival is that we know our requests are according to His will; moreover, we will be better able to keep from straying in our focus in prayer when God's words are guiding and informing us. We will learn greater boldness and confidence in praying God's words back to him, and we will find our own vision enlarged and our hope reinforced by the constant reminder that these are God's words, expressing God's desires and promises, and not merely our own.

The role of revival

> Revival days leave you with a profound realization of God's greatness and transcendence and of your own unworthiness and dependence on Him. [In this way] God accomplishes more in hours or days than usually results from

years of faithful non-revival ministry. But revival is far more than evangelism.
Man can evangelize; only God can give revival. (Dr Wesley Duewel)

So what, then, is the role of revival? This is not the place for a full discussion, but five aspects in particular may be mentioned.

Revival, in the first place, *demonstrates the power of God*. The Day of Pentecost (Acts 2) illustrates this point effectively. Luke's exciting narrative of the Spirit's descent on the waiting and expectant disciples is brief, but at its epicentre is something dynamic in the form of three supernatural signs: a sound like a violent wind, what looked like tongues of fire, and speech in other languages. Each sign proclaimed the wonders of God, the third sign – the supernatural ability to speak in a known, though hitherto not learned, language – has, in Dr John Stott's perspective a particularly fascinating aspect:

The blessing of Pentecost [is] a deliberate and dramatic reversal of the curse
of Babel. At Babel human languages were confused and the nations were
scattered; in Jerusalem the language barrier was supernaturally overcome as a
sign that the nations would now be gathered together in Christ.

In the second place, revival *exemplifies the glory of God*. But what, it may be asked, does the glory of God look like? Dr Wesley Adams puts it like this:

This is revival from heaven. When men in the streets are afraid to speak
godless words for fear that God's judgment will fall. When sinners, aware of
the fire of God's presence, tremble in the streets and cry out for mercy. When,
without human advertising, the Holy Spirit sweeps across the cities and towns
in supernatural power and holds people in the grip of terrifying conviction.
When every store [shop] becomes a pulpit, every heart an altar, every home a
sanctuary, and people walk carefully before God – this is revival.

As Dr Adams also says, this is 'the magnetism of God's presence'.

Third, revival *emphasises timeless truths about the Lord Jesus*. There is no better illustration of this than Peter's tumultuous sermon on the Day of Pentecost (Acts 2:14–41). He presents Jesus as the fulfilment of God's plan of salvation for all humanity (vv.22–24), declaring therefore that it was absolutely inconceivable that death should retain its tenacious grip on Him. This Christo-centric gospel carried with it the robust challenge to Peter's listeners to 'Repent and be baptised, every one of you, in the name [that is, the authority] of Jesus Christ for the forgiveness of your sins'. The response to this direct and unequivocal challenge was astounding: the conversion of 3,000 people – rather an impressive response to one (actually rather brief) sermon.

In the fourth place, revival *acts as a catalyst for the Church and its outreach*. It is frequently claimed that revival restores love to a loveless church, life to a moribund one, and a sense of perseverance and purpose to a disappointed and lethargic one. In a statistical sense, it is said that from 1730–45, during the Great Awakening under Jonathan Edwards, 50,000 people joined the Christian Church, while between 1857–59 the number of new Church members was a staggering 500,000.

Fifthly, revival *means days of heaven on earth*. This is an eloquent phrase coined by Dr Martyn Lloyd-Jones in his magisterial book on revival, *Revival: can we make it happen?*' He then quotes this well-known but still apposite description of what happened in 1735 in the obscure town of Northampton, Massachusetts:

> *This work soon made a glorious alteration in the town. So that in the Spring and Summer following it seemed, that is to say the town, seemed to be full of the presence of God. It never was so full of love nor so full of joy and yet so full of distress as it was then. There were remarkable tokens of God's presence in almost every house. It was a time of joy in families on account of salvation being brought to them. Parents rejoicing over their children as newborn, husbands over their wives and wives over their husbands. The doings of God were then seen in His sanctuary. God's day was a delight and His tabernacles were amiable. Our public assemblies were then beautiful. The congregation was alive in God's service. Everyone earnestly intent on the public worship. Every hearer eager to drink in the words of the minister as they came from his mouth. The assembly in general were from time to time in tears while the*

Word was preached. Some weeping with sorrow and distress, others with joy
and love, others with pity and concern for the souls of their neighbours.

Difficult questions

Revival may mean days of heaven on earth when extraordinary events take place, but a survey of revival and revivalists must also recognise that some difficult, even complex, questions need to be reflected upon in the interests of balance and an all-round approach to the subject. Three such questions will be considered here.

What are the hindrances to revival?

Today the heart's cry of many in the Church – local and worldwide – is for revival. There is an intense awareness of the great need, and a deep longing for an outpouring of the Holy Spirit that will stun the Church and the world. That the Church desperately needs a fresh demonstration of the Holy Spirit's power and anointing is incontestable and self-evident. At the same time, there are serious obstacles that render negative and ultimately frustrate the desire for a God-given move.

In attempting to reflect on the above question, reference will be made to the views of three perceptive commentators, the first being Dr Tom Phillips, a friend of Selwyn Hughes. He identifies four major obstacles. One is what he calls 'the need to know'. By this he has in mind our rationalistic, cultured, Western mindset that sees revival as a mystery that must be 'thought through', instead of viewing it as 'a movement of the Holy Spirit to be experienced with reverence and checked against the clear guidelines of Scripture, and then given to the God who alone deserves our praise'. A second is the very real personal fear of not being accepted and thus rejected by others. Dr Phillips' perceptive comment in this context is that 'In every age of conformity the thought of speaking out and standing up for God can be a truly ominous barrier'. Another potential hindrance, in his view, is apathy, which may take the form of familiarity with the extraordinary moves of the Holy Spirit (either from previous personal experience or from a historical standpoint) or a lack of interest in God's works and phenomena. A fourth hindrance is unbelief, though as Dr Phillips astutely observes 'Unbelief is not insurmountable, because the true obstacle is not collective but singular. It's me. And it's you.'

A different aspect to this whole question is provided by Richard Owen Roberts who links the obstacles in the way of revival to error-strewn preaching that is human-centred, self-exalting, non-doctrinal, without power, does not call for proper response or is, at best, a false or superficial response. In contrast, he sees preaching that promotes revival as being God-centred (exalts the God of the Bible), concerned with the glory of God, centres on the great and convicting doctrines of the Word of God, is truly empowered by the Holy Spirit, pronounces only those healings that are genuine, and demands, as did Peter's sermon on the Day of Pentecost, a radical and life-changing response from its hearers.

A third source to mention is Stephen Hill's challenging book *Time to Weep*. Formerly the evangelist at Brownsville Assembly of God Church in Pensacola, Florida, he says that the following hindrances must be dealt with before revival can possibly come: neglect of God's work of atonement, disobedience, and daily denial of God's presence: 'Most of us pretend to believe God is present everywhere, and yet we live as if He were present nowhere.'

The above comments are, admittedly, hard-hitting. They are, with some notable exceptions, realistic about the current state of the contemporary Church. Responding to hindrances is part and parcel of the preparation for revival. Now let's turn to another demanding question.

Why the phenomena?

Sensational events often occur when the Holy Spirit moves in a powerful way, with unusual – even fantastic – phenomena accompanying the public demonstrations of His power. Why?

Universal or total agreement on this contentious issue is not possible, but a constructive starting point is surely the view of Dr Martyn Lloyd-Jones, that the power of the Holy Spirit affects the 'whole person'. This is an eminently sensible and doctrinal view for the simple reason that men and women are body, soul and spirit, so that people's spiritual responses inevitably affect the soul and the body. In fact, Dr Lloyd-Jones, whose absolute acceptance of the authority of the Scriptures marked him out as one of the foremost evangelicals of the twentieth century, declared forthrightly that 'it is just folly to expect that [humanity] can react in the realm of the spiritual without anything at all happening to the rest of him' – a cause and effect argument with an overriding logical consistency from one of the most brilliant and most balanced minds ever to grapple with this thorny issue. He also viewed the manifestations as God's way of drawing attention to Himself and His work, an argument that is fully ratified and substantiated in the narratives relating to the Early Church.

On the other hand, Lloyd-Jones was insistent that the phenomena are not important in and of themselves; they should not be sought or encouraged, and certainly not boasted about, as some brand of super-Christianity, which regrettably was a tendency in some of the moves of God towards the end of the twentieth century. The antidote to such wrong thinking is to stress that desiring God's presence is the activity all Christians should be exhorted to do above everything else.

In the *Revival World Report* issue for September/October 1998, Philip Greenslade identified two errors to be avoided in the context of the phenomena. The first is depersonalising God, so that He is talked of as a power or a force, and the Holy Spirit as a 'thing' or 'it'. The second is merely being observers when unusual events occur: 'It is easy for us who may rarely, if ever, have seen displays of the Spirit's power, to feel ourselves at a long remove from the days of Pentecost and to become spectators of the Holy Spirit.' How true. In the same article, Greenslade points out that the primary function of the Holy Spirit is to illuminate Jesus to Christians; he suggests that we should take our eyes off the phenomena and fix them on Jesus because He is truly, in every sense of the word, sensational. This is not a surprise, because the Holy Spirit is the 'Spirit of truth' who brings 'glory to Jesus' (John 16:13–14).

How can we prepare for a (future) revival?

At the heart of revival is the idea of resurgence, when dead churches are reinvigorated, dormant churches become active and alive, disillusioned churches are once again infused with vision, and faithless churches become expectant and rejoicing.

On the other hand, revival doesn't simply happen. It can't be inserted into an ordinary programme, nor can it be predicted, for reasons established earlier in this introductory survey. It can, however, be prepared for – an assertion that does not in any way conflict with the view that all revivals are brought about sovereignly by God's activity, in God's timing and in God's way. Nothing, then, can manufacture genuine revival, but God's people can show Him that they are serious in their desire for a fresh awakening, to which He may respond in grace, love and mercy. Very often alongside this seriousness is the Church's realistic and humble recognition that it is 'wretched, pitiful, poor, blind and naked' (Rev. 3:17). However, neither the Church globally nor locally deserves revival, and it doesn't mean that just because we pray for revival it follows as a matter of course. If it did, it would be an act of our activity, not God's.

How, then, can individuals and whole churches prepare themselves for a dynamic move of God's power? By

+ a real commitment to prayer, on which point the history of revival is unequivocal;
+ a return to biblical preaching: in times of refreshment, God has always restored to His Church the power and value of preaching and teaching God's Word in all its seriousness and ability to convict men and women;
+ a radical cleansing. It is worth reflecting on the example of Josiah in 2 Kings 23. His actions were comprehensive and thorough, including destroying the articles made for Baal and Asherah, removing the idolatrous priests who had been burning incense to Baal, tearing down the houses where the temple prostitutes had been located, destroying the pagan altars. In today's culture, he would probably be deemed a fanatic, but it is worth remembering that as a result of his actions (not all of which are mentioned above), Israel enjoyed a significant revival in life and worship. Josiah steadfastly refused to tolerate spiritual adultery; the fact remains that revival comes when God's people earnestly want it and, crucially, are prepared to pay the price. Are we ready?

Selwyn Hughes

One man who was prepared to pay the price for a future revival was Selwyn Hughes. He was not, in the strictest definition of the word, a 'revivalist' because such a description applies to those men and women who have led revivals. He does, however, fit the description of someone who had a passionate longing for revival, and whose interest in the subject was lifelong; and I vividly recall a lengthy talk with him on the subject just a few months before he died. Another powerful reason for including him here – and one needing no apology or explanation – is that a CWR publication without reference to Selwyn would be incomplete and inadequate.

Selwyn's consciousness was, from an early age – and even before he became a Christian – formed and influenced by the Welsh Revival of 1904–05. As readers acquainted with his autobiography, *My Story*, are aware, he refers in Chapter 2 ('A Glimpse of the Future') to family gatherings when, hiding with a favourite cousin under his grandmother's capacious kitchen table, he would hear the adults discussing the events of that great spiritual awakening. The effect on him was inspirational, awakening a '[fascination] with the stories of the Welsh Revival and the more I heard the more I wanted to hear'. Selwyn recognised that moment as a door which opened, letting the future into his life.

He could not possibly have realised – or understood – in those early days that the Welsh Revival was destined to play an important, even normative, role throughout the whole of his Christian life and ministry. Often those social occasions would end with prayer meetings when Selwyn would hear his mother and father crying out in deep anguish, 'O God, do it again … do it again.' And so, indelible impressions were imprinted on his young mind of the sanctity, value and lasting significance of the Welsh Revival; something which never left him. It gave him particular pleasure many decades later to preach at the 100th Anniversary of this revival in Cardiff, when his sermon on 'The Christ of Burning, Cleansing Flame' (based on Matthew 3:11), not only impressed the gathering by the cogency and skill of his exposition, but because he was clearly a man on fire with his love for Jesus. Selwyn's two questions at the conclusion to his sermon are as powerful today as they were then: 'Is the fire of God burning in your life? Are you one of Christ's incendiaries, spreading His love and passion wherever you go?' His challenge is impossible to ignore.

Throughout his life, Selwyn was an avid and voracious reader about revival and, equally, nothing gave him greater pleasure than to preach about it. It was not a surprise, therefore, that in 1965 he should incorporate the word into the name of the vehicle (Crusade for World Revival) he chose for using his voice to pray for and believe God for a flood of His Holy Spirit in the worldwide Church. As he said himself, 'The only word I could think of to describe that was revival'. At the same time, the *Every Day with Jesus* Bible reading notes were distributed free of charge to all those who would commit themselves to *praying daily* for Holy Spirit revival, first in Britain and then the world.

Some people, including some close colleagues and friends, considered Selwyn's emphasis to be ill-timed, as the Holy Spirit was already blowing through the Church in charismatic renewal. He was not disturbed by this well-meant criticism, remaining convinced that God was calling him to elevate the spiritual vision of the Church to focus on revival, not just renewal.

This he continued to do, prayerfully and with perseverance, for the rest of his life. He wrote extensively on this theme, and the key principles of his thinking on revival are developed in *Revival: Times of Refreshing*. They are that revival is:

- an extraordinary work of God, producing extraordinary results among a large group, including physical occurrences, dynamic preaching, a defined and powerful sense of God's holiness, a clear understanding of the cross, and a deep and abiding interest in prayer and reading of the Scriptures;
- the work that God does for men and women, whereas such activities as preaching, counselling and evangelism are work that men and women do for God;
- designed primarily to bring glory to God's name, and to elevate His Church to the level of power it was always intended to enjoy. 'In such way', asserts Selwyn, 'God sends revival to arrest the attention of the world';
- comprehensive in its practical, ongoing effects: greater power and purity in the Church, God's directives become all-important, holiness becomes the prime object in the lives of Christians, along with an intense desire to see non-Christians brought into a relationship with Jesus – also, an increased love between Christians;
- frequently initiated by God when He sees that His people are serious about prayer as a preparation for revival.

Selwyn Hughes' views on revival are clear, concise, carefully crafted and biblically based. He viewed the Welsh Revival 1904–05 as the epitome of genuine revival. In several conversations with me he put forward seven reasons for this view:

1. Because it had its origins in the intense prayers of Evan Roberts – though not him alone, because in the run-up to 1904 thousands of men and women across Wales were praying for 'times of refreshment'.
2. Because it emphasised the holiness of God.
3. Because it really was a great and genuine movement of the Holy Spirit.
4. Because it released 'tremendous spiritual power throughout the Principality'.
5. Because it led to an enormous influx of people into the churches in Wales.
6. Because it radically affected society at large in hugely beneficial ways.
7. Because it resulted in at least 100,000 conversions, the vast majority during the first nine months of the outbreak.

Personal revival

Regrettably Selwyn did not ever lead a revival movement, but he did encourage and lead countless thousands of people into personal revival. This may be explained by reference to two important factors.

Through *personal example*

His influence was pervasive because from the moment of his conversion ('The most important decision of my life'), he quite simply fell in love with Jesus and, thereafter, the dominating passion of his life was to please Him in *everything* he did and thought. Let Selwyn enlarge on this statement himself:

> I met Jesus Christ when I was sixteen years of age, in South Wales. At that time I was a rugby fanatic. I was on fire about rugby, but when I met Jesus Christ and became one of His followers, I transferred the passion I had for rugby to Him and, for the past sixty years, my heart has been on fire with His love and a passion to reach the lost.

It's an obvious statement, but it needs saying: Selwyn's personal example was so powerful because he was a man of God in every sense of this dignified description. (A fuller description of his spiritual life and the governing principles of that life can be found in 7 *Laws of Spiritual Success*, first published in 2002 by CWR.)

Through *his writing*

Selwyn wrote over fifty books, though in terms of encouraging personal revival, the Bible reading notes *Every Day with Jesus* probably have pride of place. It is not an exaggeration to say that these notes have had – and continue to have – a profound effect on the experience of many, many thousands of people in Britain and, indeed, around the world, who regard them as the single most important influence on their spiritual development.

What explains the astounding success of *Every Day with Jesus*, now reaching a million readers each year? On one level its roots lie in a combination of factors, such as continuity of theme, a disciplined style, the centrality of the Scriptures, sensitive personal and pastoral concern, defined practical application and, indisputably, God's anointing. To these significant factors should be added Selwyn's understanding of the purpose of *Every Day with Jesus*: 'to get the Word into the spirit of individual believers'.

Letters continue to arrive daily at Waverley Abbey House attesting to the way these notes minister to people, helping and strengthening them, often in the bleakest and darkest of circumstances. The following poignant letter (from a Third World country) relating to the death of a young woman just after her thirtieth birthday as a result of asthma and heart failure was written by her closest friend:

> *The Lord has ministered wonderfully to us in this dark time. He particularly used you, Selwyn, to bless her family through* Every Day with Jesus. *You started the* Wilderness Experience *series for November/December and my darling friend had been studying it before she died. Her husband started reading it during the long dark nights of her illness. In fact, the* Wilderness Experience *on bereavement started on her birthday – the day before she died. All over the country, and in America and London where her relatives*

and friends were fasting and praying, we marvelled at how directly related to our situation were the words you wrote. On the Wednesday, when they [the doctors] confirmed that there was no brain activity, you talked of the wilderness of untimely death, and the first burial ceremony you conducted. On the Thursday when the life support machine was turned off, you spoke of the agony of a young man losing his wife, and having to watch all his dreams buried. Her husband says that your words greatly ministered to him and gave him courage.

There is one further aspect to mention. Men and women throughout the world have been – and are being – encouraged and personally revived by *Every Day with Jesus*. These people, should an awakening occur, will be able to respond biblically precisely because they have been taught by Selwyn to find their security and affirmation in the promises of God in His Word, not just in whatever exciting events may be happening at that moment. Selwyn consistently exhorted his readers to cultivate habits of Bible-reading, prayer and reflection, whether in revival or not. All Christians would like to be living in times of refreshment, but for the vast majority of us it simply isn't the case; which is exactly when disciplined discipleship and perseverance is vital. How grateful many of us are for the balance and care with which Selwyn taught that discipline is a vital concomitant of the Christian life as a whole.

An overview

Selwyn's whole life was dedicated to wholehearted commitment to God and His service. To the very end of his earthly pilgrimage he viewed revival, both individual and corporate, with absolute delight and seriousness. Nor is it fanciful to consider his entire life in the *context* of revival; he clung steadfastly to the concept of transformation in the life of the Church, perceiving it as 'grander and greater and more glorious than anything that can be said or written about it'. A romantic view, it might be conjectured by some, though always accompanied by realism, especially about the exaggerated claims concerning some movements in the later decades of the twentieth century: 'The very word "revival" suggests that once life existed in all its fullness, but for some reason it waned and became moribund.' Indeed.

In personal and individual terms, too, Selwyn's life was a vibrant illustration of personal ongoing revival, enabling him to face the premature deaths of his wife Enid (in 1986), his youngest son John (in December 2000), and his eldest son David (in October 2001). How did he cope? Some words from *My Story* are instructive and vibrant with deep faith and acceptance:

> *I am often asked how I coped with the loss of my two … sons within ten months of each other. I would be less than honest if I said I did not hurt. Sometimes the pain in my soul brought hot tears to my eyes. There were times when I was unable to pray, even though almost every day for close on four decades I have been forming prayers for other people to pray in the readings of* Every Day with Jesus. *… During those times when I was in so much pain that I couldn't pray I would quietly say the word 'Jesus'. In such moments God would come incredibly close to me, easing the hurt in my soul. When words fail us there is one word that never fails – Jesus.*

And, in addition, of course, there was Selwyn's own struggle with illness in the form of prostate cancer.

Selwyn Hughes continued to live the life of faith courageously and with dignity, always looking for the city that was to come (Heb. 13:14), until he died peacefully on 9 January 2006.

Notes

Quotations from the primary sources, here listed alphabetically, are gratefully acknowledged:

Robert Backhouse (ed.), *Spurgeon on Revival* (Eastbourne: Kingsway Publications, 1996).

Dr Wesley Duewel, *Revival Fire* (Grand Rapids, MI: Zondervan Publishing House, 1995).

Brian Edwards, *Revival: A People Saturated with God* (Darlington: Evangelical Press, first published 1990).

Jonathan Edwards, *The Works of Jonathan Edwards* (London, 1840).

Vernon Higham, *The Turn of The Tide* (Wheaton, Illinois: The Heath Trust and International Awakening Press, 1995).

Stephen Hill, *Time to Weep* (Florida: Creation House, 1997).

Selwyn Hughes, *Revival: Times of Refreshing* (Farnham: CWR, first published 1984).

Rhonda Hughey, *Desperate For His Presence* (Minneapolis, Minnesota: Bethany House, 2004).

Dr Martyn Lloyd-Jones, *Revival: Can we make it happen?* (London: Marshall Pickering, 1986).

T.M. Moore, *Preparing Your Church For Revival* (Fearn, Tain, Ross-shire: Christian Focus Publications, 2001).

Dr Tom Phillips, *Revival Signs* (Oregon: Vision House, 1995).

Richard Owen Roberts, *Revival* (Wheaton, Illinois: Tyndale House, 1982).

Dr John Stott, *Through the Bible; Through the Year* (Abingdon: Candle Books, 2006).

BIOGRAPHIES

TIMELINE

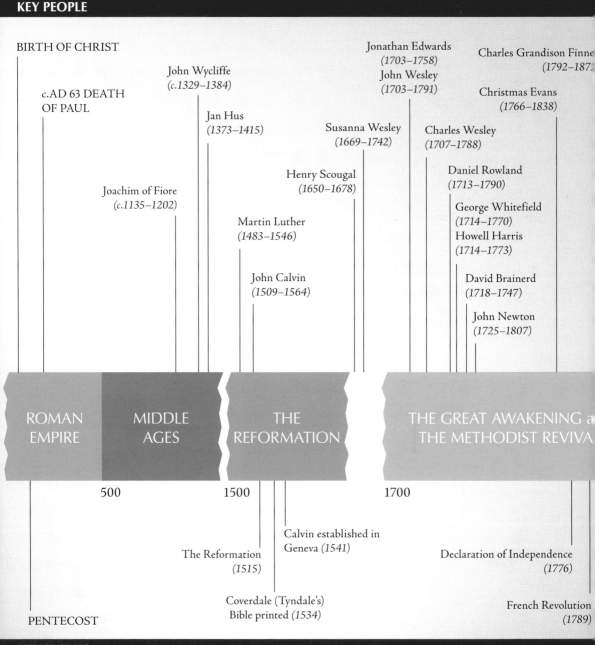

BIRTH OF CHRIST

c.AD 63 DEATH OF PAUL

John Wycliffe
(c.1329–1384)

Jan Hus
(1373–1415)

Joachim of Fiore
(c.1135–1202)

Henry Scougal
(1650–1678)

Martin Luther
(1483–1546)

John Calvin
(1509–1564)

Susanna Wesley
(1669–1742)

Jonathan Edwards
(1703–1758)

John Wesley
(1703–1791)

Charles Grandison Finne
(1792–187

Christmas Evans
(1766–1838)

Charles Wesley
(1707–1788)

Daniel Rowland
(1713–1790)

George Whitefield
(1714–1770)

Howell Harris
(1714–1773)

David Brainerd
(1718–1747)

John Newton
(1725–1807)

ROMAN EMPIRE

MIDDLE AGES

THE REFORMATION

THE GREAT AWAKENING a THE METHODIST REVIVA

500   1500   1700

The Reformation
(1515)

Calvin established in
Geneva (1541)

Coverdale (Tyndale's)
Bible printed (1534)

Declaration of Independence
(1776)

French Revolution
(1789)

PENTECOST

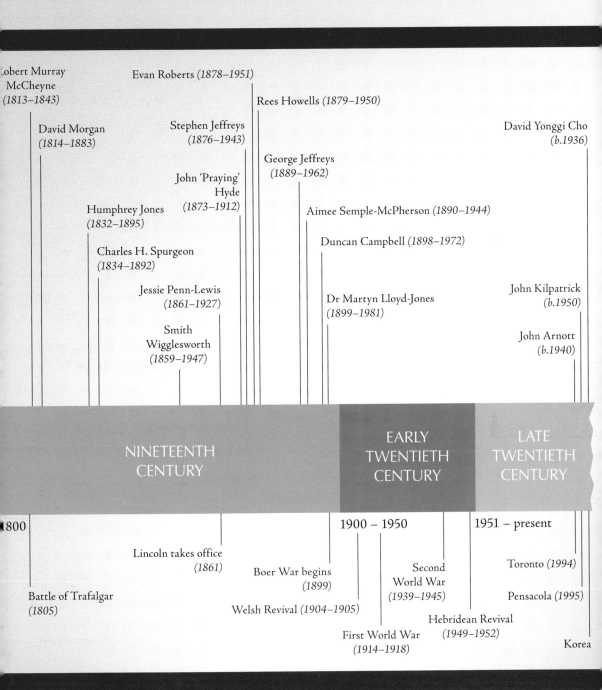

Robert Murray
McCheyne
(1813–1843)

Evan Roberts *(1878–1951)*

Rees Howells *(1879–1950)*

David Morgan
(1814–1883)

Stephen Jeffreys
(1876–1943)

David Yonggi Cho
(b.1936)

George Jeffreys
(1889–1962)

John 'Praying'
Hyde
(1873–1912)

Humphrey Jones
(1832–1895)

Aimee Semple-McPherson *(1890–1944)*

Charles H. Spurgeon
(1834–1892)

Duncan Campbell *(1898–1972)*

Jessie Penn-Lewis
(1861–1927)

Dr Martyn Lloyd-Jones
(1899–1981)

John Kilpatrick
(b.1950)

Smith
Wigglesworth
(1859–1947)

John Arnott
(b.1940)

**NINETEENTH
CENTURY**

**EARLY
TWENTIETH
CENTURY**

**LATE
TWENTIETH
CENTURY**

1800

1900 – 1950

1951 – present

Lincoln takes office
(1861)

Boer War begins
(1899)

Second
World War
(1939–1945)

Toronto *(1994)*

Battle of Trafalgar
(1805)

Pensacola *(1995)*

Welsh Revival *(1904–1905)*

Hebridean Revival
(1949–1952)

First World War
(1914–1918)

Korea

Charles Wesley

Jessie Penn-Lewis

Duncan Campbell

Rees Howells

John Newton

David Brainerd

John Wesley

George Whitefield

Susanna Wesley

Dr Martyn Lloyd-Jones

Charles Spurgeon

Charles Finney

Smith Wigglesworth

David Yonggi Cho

Aimee Semple McPherson

DAVID BRAINERD
(1718–47)

Pioneer Missionary

David Brainerd died at the age of twenty-nine. Yet whenever the associated ideas of revival and missionary endeavour and zeal are under consideration, his name is given a prominent and honourable place.

Radical conversion

The biographical facts of his life are easily chronicled. Born in 1718 in Connecticut, he was profoundly converted in 1739, later becoming a student at Yale College, one of America's foremost educational institutions. He did not last very long there, however, and he was expelled for what Jonathan Edwards later described as 'intemperate, indiscreet zeal'. Some time after this he was licensed to preach and was appointed by The Scottish Society for the Propagation of Christian Knowledge to be their missionary to the Delaware Indians of North America, an assignment which became his life's work. It was to involve Brainerd in living the rest of his life in Eastern Pennsylvania under conditions of severe hardship until finally disease got the better of him.

True disciple

The external facts of his life may be scanty, but his qualities as a man of God shine out radiantly, constituting a stirring example for all Christians today. Not for him the almost continuous grumbling that characterises so many churches in the contemporary evangelical scene. Three positive qualities in particular stand out.

In the first place, he was supremely a *man of prayer*. He shares this dedication to a holy life with all those whom God has used in revival, including Robert Murray McCheyne, Wesley, Whitefield and Evan Roberts. It was not unusual for Brainerd to spend whole nights in prayer seeking for the touch of a supernatural God in order to be equipped and anointed for service. His example confirms a vital spiritual principle: there are no short cuts (or instant answers) to spiritual maturity or effectiveness in God's service.

In the second place, he *delighted himself in God*. An entry in his diary for 12 July 1739 shows an intensity in his appreciation of God:

> As I was walking in a dark, thick grove, unspeakable glory seemed to open to the view and apprehension of my soul. I do not mean any external brightness, for I saw no such thing, nor do I intend any imagination of any body of light somewhere in the third heaven or anything of that nature, but it was a new inward apprehension or view that I had of God, such as I never had before, nor anything which had the least semblance of it. I stood still, wondered and admired! I knew that I never had seen before anything comparable to it for excellency and beauty, it was widely different from all the conceptions that ever I had of God or things Divine. I had no particular apprehension of any one Person in the Trinity, either the Father, the Son, or the Holy Ghost, but it appeared to be Divine Glory. My soul rejoiced with joy unspeakable *to see* such a God, such a glorious Divine Being, and I was inwardly pleased and

satisfied that He should be God over all for ever and ever. My soul was so captivated and delighted with the excellency, loveliness, greatness, and other perfections of God, that I was even swallowed up in Him.

In the third place, he valued highly and *practised holiness*. This followed almost inevitably from the personal revelation quoted above, and again his diary gives a clear insight into the man and the burning convictions that motivated him:

All things here below vanished, and there appeared to be nothing of any considerable importance to me but holiness of heart and life, and the conversion of the heathen to God. All my cares, fears, and desires, which might be said to be of a worldly nature disappeared, and were, in my esteem, of little more importance than a puff of wind. I exceedingly longed that God would get to himself a name among the heathen, and I appealed to him, with the greatest freedom, that he knew I 'preferred him above my chief joy'.

Here was a man, as Brian Edwards says in his book *Revival: A People Saturated with God*, whom God could trust in revival. David Brainerd served God in the harshest and most unpromising of circumstances, a bleak and hostile environment that frequently drove him to the edge of despair. That he was able to continue was due to an unshakeable conviction that he had been specially called to take the gospel to the Indians of North America; his own indomitable spirit that was daily refreshed and uplifted in prayer, enabling him to ride at least 3,000 miles on horseback; and his passion for those who did not know God in personal ways.

... he valued highly and *practised holiness.*

Product of revival

He was himself the product of revival. He journeyed almost 500 miles to the Susquehannah Indians, amongst whom a great revival erupted. His wholehearted dedication to the conversion of these people is clearly mirrored in his diary: 'All things

33

here below vanished and there appeared to be nothing of any importance to me but holiness of heart and the conversion of the heathen to God.'

Sacrificial lifestyle

Such was Brainerd's devotion that the abiding image, enshrined in history, is of him praying in the snow until it melted around him and was stained with his blood. Prevail in prayer for revival he certainly did until his death on 9 October 1747.

Challenge for today

A curious fact about revival history is that Brainerd, like Robert Murray McCheyne and Ann Griffiths (the eighteenth-century Welsh hymnist) died before reaching the age of thirty. And yet, their influence resonates powerfully in the twenty-first century. Why? In Brainerd's case, it is because of his holiness and passion for men and women to come into a personal relationship with Jesus.

Brainerd's life demonstrated that there is no easy route to spiritual maturity. It requires discipline and thoughtfulness that have their source in a love relationship with Jesus, and the robustness to withstand difficulties and opposition. Brainerd's life eloquently illustrated these qualities, and he poses a challenge to us as we live in these more self-indulgent times.

Prayer

O God, forgive us for our frequent laziness, even apathy, in Your service. We desperately need Your strength to be effective witnesses to Your love and compassion for everyone. Amen.

DUNCAN CAMPBELL

(1898–1972)

Revivalist and man of God

Duncan Campbell was born at the end of the nineteenth century. He died in 1972. His life and work were almost immediately honoured (in 1974) by the publication of Andrew Woolsey's biography, *Duncan Campbell, A Biography: The Sound of Battle*. Today he is largely remembered as the human face of the Hebridean Revival (1949–52), later as the principal of the Faith Mission Bible College, and for *Revivalist and Man of God Duncan Campbell*, his perceptive insight into the whole process of revival, which he defined – simply and memorably – as 'a community saturated with God', so that men and women (again in his own words) 'are powerfully awakened to eternal realities and become concerned about their salvation, or the salvation of friends and neighbours'.

Man of God

This profile is not concerned with his key role in the Hebrides midway through the twentieth century, instead it is with his qualities as a man of God. Gaelic-speaking and living amidst the rugged grandeur of the Scottish Highlands as a child, his life was quite literally transformed by his conversion. He recalls that momentous event unpretentiously though humorously:

> I well remember the prayer that I offered. It was in Gaelic (I'm so thankful that God understands Gaelic): 'Lord, I know not what to do. I know not how to come, but if You'll take me as I am, I'm coming now!' I was saved with God's eternal salvation.

From that moment onwards and until the end of his life, God was a burning reality to Duncan Campbell. He had encountered the living God and was radically changed.

Uncompromising

The word most frequently used by contemporaries about Duncan Campbell was 'uncompromising'. There was a ruggedness and a determination about him that set him apart from even his fellow Christians. He was uncompromising in his:

+ *Pursuit of God*. He sought God for Himself, surely a product of that first meeting with Him at conversion. God was, for Duncan Campbell, the supreme reality of his life, and he was determined to be an obedient follower, whatever the cost. It was this uncompromising attitude which marked him out as the future leader of the revival in the Hebrides.
+ *Preaching*. He was totally unafraid in his preaching of the gospel, about which there was nothing complicated or fancy. As his biographer says, it was without fear; Campbell exposed sin in its ugliness, dwelling at length on the consequences of living and dying without the Lord Jesus Christ. Campbell's preaching was prophetic, not diplomatic, and his hearers were called to make a clear choice; it was a solemn thought to him that the eternity of those who heard him might turn upon his faithfulness.
+ *Lifestyle*. It wasn't just that Duncan Campbell was a non-smoker, a total abstainer

and hated dancing, his whole desire was to be surrendered to God in the very manner of his daily life. Holiness was, to him, a matter of living as God wants us to live – no more, no less. He was a warm-hearted man, full of integrity, but also of love for those who needed to find the love of God demonstrated so supremely in Jesus Christ. It is said of him that he was 'full of Christ', an accolade few Christians merit.

- *Prayer life*. He was, in a very real sense, a prayer warrior. Before undertaking any engagement he would pray, and also enlist the aid of similarly committed people. Not surprisingly, some of the most dramatic outpourings on the Hebrides occurred when he was asked to pray. One night in the police station at Barvas, he only said one word, 'Father', and all those present were melted to tears as God's tangible presence invaded the whole building. Throughout his life, Duncan Campbell rose each day at 6.00am so that he could pray before starting to deal with the other demands of the day. It was thus that he was refreshed and equipped for all that lay ahead of him. At the Faith Mission Bible College, every Friday afternoon was given over to prayer and waiting upon God. On such occasions the students and staff felt, in the words of a former student, that they 'were standing on Holy ground'.

> God was the supreme reality of his life …

Fighting on

The four qualities outlined above marked him out as a man of God. But how was he enabled to keep going, often in debilitating weakness? Some of his oft-repeated emphases provide the explanation. 'No victory is secure,' he said, 'except by greater victories'; and in his last message he exhorted: 'Keep on fighting, but see that you are fighting in the love of Christ.' The first quotation pinpoints his determination not to be a prisoner of the past (however glorious); rather, using the past as a springboard for victories to come, he faced the future resolutely. And the next quotation highlights his intense commitment to be a soldier in the service of Jesus Christ. He considered such service a huge privilege.

Duncan Campbell made a daily and unequivocal response to the sound of battle until 20 March 1972, when he died at the School of Evangelism in Lausanne. His memory is an inspiration to all who wish to see God once again sweeping through Britain and the world in revival power.

Challenge for today

Duncan Campbell was the human face of the last revival in Britain, a movement that he memorably characterised as God 'sweeping in'. To Campbell, revival had nothing whatsoever to do with organisations (however skilful), with personal gifting (however remarkable), but everything to do with God's activity first and last. It is a message that needs stressing afresh in our generation.

The indispensable key to Campbell's ministry was his willingness to surrender his life totally to God. He was prepared to pay the price for revival. A contemporary once said Campbell was 'full of Christ'. Now, that is a challenge (and possibly a rebuke?) to us all.

Prayer

Father, help us to realise that serving You is a privilege and an honour – in fact, the greatest in the world. Strengthen our resolve so that we serve You devotedly and determinedly in today's world. Amen.

JONATHAN EDWARDS
(1703–58)

Revivalist and scholar

J onathan Edwards is commonly regarded as the greatest revivalist of
all time. His reputation as a philosopher and theologian is higher
today than it has ever been and, over 200 years after his death, he
continues to exercise considerable influence on the thought-life of
America and over all those countries for which the concept of revival
is significant.

He was a truly remarkable man, his name being inseparably
linked with the Great Awakening that broke out in Northampton,
Massachusetts in 1735 and continued later, in 1740, with the visit of
George Whitefield.

The facts

Born in Connecticut, New England, Jonathan Edwards was the
only son of Timothy Edwards, pastor at East Windsor. Marked
out early as a person of high intelligence and precocious ability, he
was converted at seventeen as he read, 'Now unto the King eternal,

immortal, invisible, the only wise God, be honour and glory for ever and ever. Amen' (1 Tim. 1:17, AV). He described the experience like this:

> There came into my soul … a sense of the glory of the Divine Being; a new sense, quite different from anything I had ever experienced before … from about that time I began to have a new kind of apprehension and ideas of Christ, and the work of redemption, and the glorious way of salvation.

Three years later, on 12 January 1723, he made, in his own words,

> A solemn declaration of myself to God, and wrote it down; giving up myself, and all that I had to God; to be for the future, in no respect my own; to act as one that had no right to be himself, in any respect.

Edwards was both a graduate of, and tutor at, Yale but in 1727 he became the associate pastor of the Congregational Church at Northampton, the location of the Great Awakening of 1735. His view of that tumultuous period is enshrined in *A Faithful Narrative of the Surprising Work of God*. He draws attention to the astonishing number of conversions, the love and joy that characterised both the recent converts and the established Christians, and the fact that 'There was scarcely a single person in the town, old or young, left unconcerned about the great things of the eternal world'. The overall effect on the town of Northampton was quite remarkable: 'It seems to be a time of joy in families on account of salvation being brought unto them; parents rejoicing over their children as new born, and husbands over their wives, and wives over their husbands.'

The theologian of experience

This heading is Dr Lloyd-Jones' description of Jonathan Edwards (*The Puritans*, pp.348–71), and any portrait of him must give due and appropriate emphasis to three aspects in particular. First, his 'balanced thinking'. Blessed with a towering intellect and a brilliantly creative imagination, Edwards submitted everything to the verdict and assessment of Scripture: 'Everything,' as Lloyd-Jones says, 'was subordinate to the Word of God.' Even after all this time his passionate devotion to God, his genuinely humble posture and the brilliance of his mind all shine through powerfully and influentially for modern Christians. The sheer sense of integration and wholeness is clearly apparent.

Second, his view of true religion. Quite simply he saw it as an affair of the heart, a living, vibrant meeting with God that transcended all other aspects of his life. Listen to his description of an experience he had in 1737:

> *Having alighted from my horse in a retired place, as my manner commonly had been, to walk for divine contemplation and prayer, I had a view that for me was extraordinary, of the glory of the Son of God, as Mediator between God and man, and his wonderful, great, full, pure and sweet grace and love, and meek and gentle condescension. This grace that appeared so calm and sweet, appeared also great above the heavens.*

Third, his preaching. It was expository, analytical and applied. His preaching was never merely a dissertation or an address, it was directed at influencing his hearers' minds, hearts and consciences. His dominating interest was the truth about God and His actions in history, so that those listening were informed, stimulated and challenged to put the eternal truths into action in their everyday lives. He argued persuasively for both light and heat in preaching, theology on fire if you wish, once again demonstrating the balance that so marked out his whole life. His preaching was also characterised by a disciplined thoroughness and, as Colin Whittaker says, 'He did all within his power to ensure that each person passed through a true repentance into the experience of the new birth' (*Great Revivals*, p.26).

The eternal truths taught in the Bible were the springboard for his life and ministry.

Jonathan Edwards' life is significant for many reasons, including the need for Spirit-filled preaching, holy living, and the paramount importance of the Bible for all aspects of life and godliness. It also reminds us of the surpassing need for revival, for an outpouring of the Holy Spirit in convicting power. Lord, do it again, we pray.

Challenge for today

Edwards was a phenomenally gifted person as a theologian and philosopher, a graduate of Yale University, but he realised and taught uncompromisingly that God's immediate presence was much more important. Do we?

The eternal truths taught in the Bible were the springboard for his life and ministry – not publicity, not materialism, not denominational considerations, but the reality of God as demonstrated in His Word.

Edwards challenges us today to place all our gifts at God's disposal and direction.

Prayer

O God, we thank You for the gifts of intellect and personality You have given Your followers. Help us to use them in wisdom and in a way that reflects our love for You and brings You glory. Amen.

CHRISTMAS EVANS

(1766–1838)

The Bunyan of Wales

Christmas Evans is a largely neglected figure nowadays. It's all so different from the nineteenth century when he was widely regarded as one of the three greatest preachers in Wales, the other two being John Elias (1774–1841) and William Williams of Wern.

Early days

Born on Christmas Day 1766, the son of a cobbler, his early life was humble and his education informal and rudimentary. In 1789, however, he was ordained into the Baptist ministry, serving between 1791–1826 in his beloved Anglesey. There followed two pastorates in South Wales (in Caerphilly and Cardiff) before he returned home to Caernarvon, where he spent the remaining years of his life.

Ordinary but influential

It is clear that in purely external terms, Christmas Evans' life was ordinary, simple even; certainly unremarkable. In terms of his influence, especially in North Wales, he was a spiritual giant, so much so that the Puritan Conference of 1967 declared him to be the 'greatest preacher the Baptists have ever had in Great Britain'.

Such forthright contentions are always difficult to substantiate, still less to prove beyond doubt, but of his qualities as a man and as a servant of God there is considerable certainty.

Firstly, Evans was an *able communicator* in an age long before the technical aids so readily available today. Publicity before big events was unknown, but his appearances at the Baptist Association meetings created great excitement. One such occasion has been described as follows:

> *So, along all the roads, there presses an untiring crowd, showing that something unusual is going on somewhere. The roads are all picturesque and lively with all sorts of people, on foot, on horseback, in old farm carts, and even in carriages; all wending their way to the largest and most central chapel of the neighbourhood. It is the chief service. It is a Sabbath evening; the congregation is wedged together in the spacious house of God; it becomes almost insupportable, but the Welsh like it. The service has not commenced, and a cry is already raised that it had better be held in an adjoining field; but it is said this would be inconvenient. The doors, the windows, are all thrown open; and so the time goes on, and the hour for the commencement of the service arrives. All eyes are strained as the door opens beneath the pulpit, and the Minister of the congregation comes in, and makes his way, as well as he can, for himself and his friend, the great preacher.*

Then, secondly, he was *deeply prayerful* in his whole approach to the ministry. He wrote himself:

The spirit of energetic supplication was given to me early. A sense of danger prompts the soul to seek deliverance. Earnestness in prayer grew with me, though I frequently feared it would become extinct. Still, it was not entirely extinquished, even in those days of darkness when I but barely perceived that the merits of Christ were the only plea, without reference to anything of our own. After I came to know and feel that the righteousness of Christ formed the only ground to be depended upon before God, I was able with every sense of unworthiness to approach Him with a stronger expectation. The Christian must have a rock in the merits of the Redeemer to rest upon; and here he finds 'a place of refuge, and a covert from the storm and the rain'.

From this quotation it is possible to perceive him as a humble dedicated servant of Christ, with absolute confidence in Christ and His righteousness, and someone who knew where to find refuge and help in the darkest of circumstances.

Perhaps, above all, Christmas Evans was an unusual and dramatic preacher. His method of preaching was, in essence, allegorical, earning for him the sobriquet of 'the Bunyan of Wales'; and his style of preaching is clearly apparent from the following extract (quoted in *Christmas Evans*, by B.A. Ramsbottom):

Saul of Tarsus and his Seven Ships

Saul of Tarsus was once a thriving merchant and an extensive shipowner. He had seven vessels of his own: the names of which were – 'Circumcised the eighth day'; 'Of the stock of Israel'; 'Of the tribe of Benjamin'; 'An Hebrew of the Hebrews'; 'As touching the law, a Pharisee'; 'Concerning zeal, persecuting the church'; 'Touching the righteousness which is of the law, blameless'. The sixth was a man-of-war with which he set out one day from the port of Jerusalem, well supplied with ammunition from the arsenal of the chief priest,

His effectiveness was closely related to his determination to ensure that God received the glory for everything that happened.

with a view to destroy a small fort at Damascus.

He was wonderfully confident, and breathed out threatenings and slaughter.

But he had not gone far from port before the Gospel ship, with Jesus Christ

Himself as commander on board, hove in sight, and threw such a shell among

the merchant's fleet that all his ships were instantly on fire. The commotion

was tremendous; and there was such a volume of smoke that Saul couldn't

see the sun at noon.

While the ships were fast sinking, the Gospel commander mercifully gave

orders that the perishing merchant should be taken on board. 'Saul, Saul, what

has become of thy ships?' 'They are on fire!' 'What wilt thou do now?' 'O that

I may be found in Him, not having mine own righteousness, which is of the

law, but that which is through the faith of Christ, the righteousness which is of

God by faith.'

As one modern theologian has aptly remarked, Evans' preaching 'was attended by divine power', without which, of course, revival will never come.

Challenge for today

Evans was an eloquent illustration of an ordinary man whom God used to achieve great things. He became, under God's guidance, an able, fluent communicator of the gospel, and a powerful preacher.

In fact, the Holy Spirit equipped him to become one of the greatest preachers in the glorious history of Welsh revivals. His effectiveness was closely related to his determination to ensure that God received the glory for everything that happened.

Prayer

Heavenly Father, we long for divine power to be manifest in our meetings so that we step out of the rut into revival. You can rend the heavens again, and we beseech You to do it. We are Your servants. Amen.

CHARLES GRANDISON FINNEY
(1792–1875)

Theologian of revival

Charles Grandison Finney was a man of many talents. At different times, he was a lawyer, pastor, professor and college president, but it is as a revivalist that he is best remembered today on both sides of the Atlantic. A native of Connecticut, he was the seventh child of farming parents who had migrated westward with many other young families in post-Revolutionary America. Educated at Oneida Academy in Clinton, the original intention was that he should proceed to Yale College, but that plan fell through and he subsequently trained for the legal profession in New York.

Converted and redirected

In October 1821, however, his life took a dramatic turn when he was converted, thus changing the entire direction of his life, and he left the law in order to train for the Presbyterian ministry. Ordination followed three years later. From the very start of his ministry, he emphasised the rock-like authority of the Bible, the paramount need for conversion and, post-conversion, the duty of disciplined, daily commitment to the Lord Jesus Christ. His overwhelming concern throughout his life was the conversion of men and women who would then prepare wholeheartedly for the coming of God's kingdom on earth.

Dynamic preaching

Between 1824–31, he worked energetically in upstate New York, Connecticut and many other places to bring people under the influence of the life-transforming gospel of Jesus Christ, and it is estimated that approximately a quarter of a million people were converted as a result of his preaching. But it is as a leader of evangelical revivalism that Charles Finney is primarily remembered today. This is so not only because of his pioneering preaching but also because of his *Lectures on Revivals in Religion* which were published in 1835, by which time he was Professor of Theology at Oberlin Collegiate Institute, Ohio.

These lectures, delivered originally at the Chatham Street Chapel, New York, probably constitute the most exhaustive treatment of the subject of revival. As Donald Dayton says in his introduction to *Reflections on Revival*,

> They have guided generations of Christians and evangelists seeking revival in their churches. Today, over a century and a half later, they are still studied and treasured. Even those who do not share Finney's faith study this work to understand the development of American church life and culture.

Ten years later (1845), Finney wrote a series of letters on revivals which contain his mature reflections on the subject. For a considered view of Finney it is necessary to consult both volumes, together with the various biographies of his life and ministry.

Controversial

Finney's biographers are united in stressing his intense prayer life, his willingness to respond to change – and changing ideas – in a positive and constructive way, and his radical insistence on practical and immediate holiness. He was also keenly interested in social reform, insisting that it was impossible to be on the right side of God and on the wrong side of slavery (quoted in *Revival: Principles to Change the World*, by Winkie Pratney); and his hatred of slavery made him one of the most impressive Christian revolutionaries in nineteenth-century America. His biographers also stress the *astonishing impact* of his preaching; they compare the opening of his mouth to the aiming of a gun, and the accompanying bombardment. Hardly surprisingly, the combination of these factors (especially his uncompromising stand on the truths of the gospel and his unbending attitude to social abuses) made him a controversial figure, and he was the target for much criticism from other preachers and Church figures who did not agree with his radical views.

How do revivals start?

Finney's views on revival too caused – and still continue to cause – controversy. In particular, they concerned his ideas regarding the starting of revivals. As Brian Edwards says in *Revival: A People Saturated with God*,

> He firmly believed that revivals could be produced by following a set of rules. He followed his own rules and was very effective. There was a great movement and many lives were changed, but how far it was a true revival is a subject historians still argue about.

> To glorify Jesus was the heartbeat of Finney's life.

Certainly many commentators would take exception to Finney's insistence that a revival can be 'promoted' (chapter 3 of his *Lectures on Revivals*), just like any other evangelistic initiative; as indeed they would to his claim that revivals could be 'guaranteed', if only the right conditions were created. It is not appropriate in a brief profile like this to comment extensively on the various theories of revival, though it is worth asserting that revival is always a sovereign act of God, whatever the circumstances, whatever the declension in the Church and its chronic divisions, and that revival, in Dr Martyn

Lloyd-Jones' words, 'Above everything else, is a glorification of the Lord Jesus Christ, the Son of God. It is the restoration of him to the centre of the life of the Church' (*Revival: Can we make it happen?*, p.47).

Qualities and influence

Charles Finney was a man of *courage* (facing his detractors resolutely), *consistency* (once he discovered the gospel, he spent his life proclaiming it), and *absolute devotion* to the Lord Jesus. He had faults, too, not least his proneness to express himself in excessively emotive and extravagant language. His place in the history of revival, however, is secure – some would say unrivalled – and his *Lectures* continue to have considerable influence on people today: witness the many, many times his words have been quoted in articles on the 'Toronto Blessing' since 1994. He died peacefully in Oberlin on 16 August 1875, after a lifetime's energetic endeavour, the words on his grave posing a challenge for us all: 'The Lord be with you as He was with our fathers: let us not fail nor forsake Him.'

Challenge for today

Known universally as the theologian of revival, Finney's overwhelming passion was for men and women to come to know Jesus Christ in personal, transforming ways. So, one of the challenges from his life for us today is to seek Jesus first, not revival, not for His blessings, but for Himself. Like Mary (Luke 10:39), we are asked to sit at Jesus' feet listening to what he says.

To glorify Jesus was the heartbeat of Finney's life. It was the principle on which his whole life was built.

Prayer

O Lord, we thank You for Finney's life and insights into revival, but we thank You most of all for Your beloved Son, Jesus. Enable us to serve Him with all our minds and bodies. Amen.

HOWELL HARRIS
(1714–73)

Sold out for God

Evangelism is invariably the work of revival. But it is evangelism of a particular sort – a desperate concern amounting to a passion. This passion characterised Howell Harris, the principal founder of Welsh Calvinistic Methodism and a key figure in the eighteenth-century revival that swept through the Principality with such powerful and healing effect. The result was that society was transformed. Churches increased in numbers, and the gospel proved irresistible, all of which we long for today.

Humble origins

Born in Talgarth, Brecon in ordinary, indeed humble, circumstances, Harris very early in life expressed the desire to become an ordained minister in the established Church. It was not to be, however, and in 1735 his life took a decisive and radical change. This is what happened. Attending the communion service in Talgarth Parish Church on Palm Sunday – 30 March – he came under a powerful conviction of sin, which left him in an agony of mind and spirit. Almost two months later, on 25 May, Whit Sunday, while attending another communion service in the same church, he found real, tangible and lasting peace. He said,

> At the table, Christ bleeding on the Cross was kept before my eyes constantly; and strength was given to me to believe that I was receiving pardon on account of that blood. I lost my burden; I went home leaping for joy (Practice of Piety, first published in 1611).

Harris had been thoroughly and profoundly converted, and this experience changed the whole direction of his future life and the subsequent course of his public ministry. He had become, in Dr Martyn Lloyd-Jones' words, 'A flaming Evangelist who felt a compassion for souls and a sorrow for all people who were in sin.'

Spiritual barrenness

Harris's example and that of his contemporary Daniel Rowland (1713–90) was sorely needed, for at this time Wales and Britain, as a whole, were in a spiritual state of decline, with ignorance apparent on every hand. Morally the country was degenerate, with drunkenness a social curse. It is against this background of moral laxity and an impoverished Church that Harris's work and ministry must be viewed, especially his wholehearted and passionate preaching of the gospel and his role in the revival of the eighteenth century.

The man

But what sort of a man was Howell Harris? Admittedly shy and awkward in human terms, he was essentially a man of integrity and holiness who maintained an intimate walk with God. One entry in his diary is sufficient to illustrate this fact. This is what he wrote for 18 June 1735, thus not long after his conversion:

Being in secret prayer, I felt suddenly my heart melting within me, like wax before the fire, with love for God my Saviour. I felt not only love and peace, but also a longing to be dissolved and to be with Christ; and there was a cry in my inmost soul, with which I was totally unacquainted before.

Harris also brought to the work of preaching and revival considerable energy and courage. He was quite often in grave physical danger from antagonistic crowds opposed to the public presentation of the gospel, and he narrowly escaped being murdered on at least one notable occasion.

Binding all these qualities together, however, was his *spirituality*. As Dr Martyn Lloyd-Jones said, 'Harris lived in the realm of the Spirit being sensitive to the Holy Spirit's influences.'

Looking back

Harris's life was not without its problems and difficulties. Most notably, there were theological controversies with Rowland and Whitefield regarding the rival claims of Calvinism and Arminianism, but nothing can detract from, or dim, his deep devotion to God, his unquenchable belief in God's sovereignty, and his undiminished delight in the preaching of the good news of God's grace in Jesus Christ. Harris died on 21 July 1773, having faced his end with confidence and faith. Truly an individual saturated with God.

> Harris lived in the realm of the Holy Spirit more consistently than most people.

Challenge for today

As the subtitle to this biography implies, Harris lived in the realm of the Holy Spirit more consistently than most people. His passionate devotion to preaching the gospel is one that all contemporary preachers need to face honestly and resolutely. Preaching was not, for Harris, a part-time or optional activity. It consumed him utterly. Why? Because he was utterly convinced of the reality of the truths he spoke about. Not for him the prosperity gospel so beloved of some today, rather the gospel of God's saving grace in rescuing sinners from the consequences of their sin.

Before preaching, Harris disciplined himself to hear from God first. As Jack Deere says in *Surprised by the Voice of God*, the divine pattern for all Christian ministry is illustrated in the life of Jesus who '... heard from his Father before he did or said things. Jesus didn't originate this pattern, but he fulfilled it on a far grander scale than anyone could have ever imagined.' Long years before the twenty-first century, Howell Harris understood this principle which, surely, is the normative pattern for our lives (and ministries) today.

Prayer

O God, help us to be so attuned to Your voice that the Word and the Spirit operate dynamically in our lives – in my life – so that, like Howell Harris, we accurately reflect what You wish to say to our world. Amen.

REES HOWELLS
(1879–1950)

Wrestling in prayer

Rees Howells was a perfectly ordinary man whose story is known to millions throughout the world. This is largely as a result of Norman Grubb's biography, *Rees Howells: Intercessor*.

Born on 10 October 1879 in Brynaman, South Wales, he was the sixth in a family of eleven children. Hardly surprisingly, life was tough for the Howells family, a situation made worse by the horrors of unemployment. They were, though, a happy family, 'for godliness and love were pre-eminent in the house', according to Grubb. There were also clear links with revival because Rees' grandparents had been converted in the Welsh Revival of 1859.

Leaving school at the age of twelve, Rees was an ironworker for ten years before emigrating to America where a cousin procured for him a job in the mining industry. At this stage, however, Rees Howells was not a Christian, but at the age of twenty-three – and brought on by a near fatal attack of typhoid fever – he realised that to die without faith in Jesus Christ meant, in Norman Grubb's words, 'separation from God for ever'. Encountering the preaching of Maurice Reuben, a converted Jew, in Connellsville, Pennsylvania, Rees himself records: 'I was born into another world. I found myself in the kingdom of God, and the Creator became my Father.'

Returning to Wales, Rees found the whole country under the power and presence of the Holy Spirit, but it was not until 1906, in Llandrindod Wells, that he was brought to a position of unconditional surrender to God. As he said: 'Nothing is more real to me.' Love of money, pride, ambition and self-awareness were dealt with, purged and expunged, and henceforth Rees Howells was dedicated utterly and totally to God's service. Central to this life of obedience and intercession was 'being willing for the Holy Spirit to live through him the life the Saviour would have lived, if He had been in his place.'

In 1915, Rees and Elizabeth Howells (whom he had married in 1910) left for Africa to work with the South Africa General Mission in Gazaland, close to the border with what is now Mozambique. What happened there was nothing less than a huge outpouring of the Holy Spirit, with all forty-three mission stations experiencing revival.

Having returned to Wales in 1920, Rees Howells discovered the need for a Bible college to prepare men and women for Christian service and, in 1924, the Bible College of Wales, Swansea, was opened, with Rees as its first director. For the next sixteen years he gave himself to the ministry (unseen but vitally important) of intercession for a global outpouring of the Holy Spirit.

A particularly striking instance of his life of intercession concerned the impending outbreak of the Second World War. Initially Howells believed that God would intervene and prevent the war. When that was obviously not going to happen, he published a statement on 4 September 1939 which said:

> The Lord has made known to us that He is going to destroy Hitler and the Nazi regime, that the world may know that it was God and God alone who has scattered the dictators. Three and a half years ago, the College prayed this prayer for weeks and months, and we firmly believe He will now answer it. He has isolated Germany so that He may get at this evil system, which is

the Antichrist, and release Germany, the land of the Reformation. He will deal with the Nazis as He dealt with the Egyptian army in the time of Moses. God will cause Hitler to fall on the battlefield or by a mutiny or a great rising in Germany against the Nazis.

He was not shaken by war. Typically he redoubled his prayers for the nation, in which context Norman Grubb's comment is entirely appropriate:

> *When we look back now after these years, many of us in Britain recall the terror of those days. Remembering the miracle of Dunkirk, acknowledged by our leaders to be an intervention from God, the calm sea allowing the smallest boats to cross, the almost complete evacuation of our troops, and then the lead Mr Churchill gave to the nation, how thankful we are that God had this company of hidden intercessors, whose lives were on the altar day after day as they stood in the gap for the deliverance of Britain.*

Rees Howells' life as an intercessor continued unabated until his death on 13 February 1950.

Challenge for today

Rees Howells' life challenges men and women whose Christian lives are tepid and lukewarm. His devotion to the Lord Jesus was, according to his contemporaries, like a furnace, and it is no exaggeration to say that Howells was totally dedicated to God and His people.

As the first director of the Swansea Bible College, he exhorted his students to make a full commitment to Jesus, pointing out to them that the only possible route to such an allegiance was through the purging fire of the Holy Spirit. He was an intercessor who, like Jacob in Genesis 32, wrestled in prayer, for himself, his family, his college and the nation of Britain. He also prayed for worldwide revival. Howells

He was an intercessor who ... wrestled in prayer, for himself, his family, his college and the nation of Britain.

experienced revival himself in Africa with the South African General Mission in Gazaland, and that experience burned within him for the rest of his ministry.

Prayer

Lord Jesus, You gave Your life for us, and You call us today to similarly lay down our lives for You. Such a prospect causes fear to rise within us, but we know that You are able to conquer those fears. Make us men and women of courage, we pray. Amen.

JOHN 'PRAYING' HYDE
(1873–1912)

Prayer and the sanctified life

John Hyde, the American Presbyterian missionary, who died on 17 February 1912, is universally referred to in the history of the Church as 'Praying Hyde of India'.

Deeply committed

He was one of six children born into a deeply committed Christian family. His father, Smith Harris Hyde was, for seventeen years, the minister of the Presbyterian Church in Carthage, Illinois, and his mother was a gentle, sweet-tempered, music-loving person.

India

After undergraduate training at McCormack Theological Seminary, Hyde sailed for India in 1892. This was at a time in history of much missionary activity: prayer circulars were being sent from India to Britain, America and Australia to mobilise intercession for India.

Each Saturday afternoon for eleven years, ministers and laymen in Melbourne, Australia, banded together to pray for revival there and around the world.

Two significant developments in Hyde's life at this point included a fresh infilling of the Holy Spirit, and his decision to give priority to prayer in his life, praying specifically for revival. Four years later, he felt convinced that God had acceded to his request to be 'a real Israel, a wrestler with God' (quoted in Basil Miller's book, *Praying Hyde*, published in 1943). By 1899, it was not uncommon for him to spend whole nights in prayer, prevailing on God for a dynamic manifestation of divine power. Then, in 1904, Hyde and a number of other missionaries established the 'Punjab Prayer Union', designed to pray for revival in the Punjab in particular, and for India as a whole.

Revival

In late August 1904, Christian workers from all denominations gathered at Saikot in the Punjab. Before this convention, John Hyde and R. McCheyne Paterson prayed, waited and tarried one whole month before the opening date. Something of the intensity of their prayer lives is encapsulated in Francis A. McGaw's account (he was one of Hyde's fellow-workers):

> For thirty days and thirty nights these godly men waited before God in prayer. Do we wonder that there was power in the convention? Turner joined them after nine days, so that for twenty-one days and twenty-one nights these three men prayed and praised God for a mighty outpouring of His power. Three human hearts that beat as one and that won the heart of Christ, yearning, pleading, crying, and agonising over the Church of India and the myriads of lost souls. Three renewed human wills that by faith linked themselves as with hooks of steel to the omnipotent will of God. Three pairs of fire-touched lips that out of believing hearts shouted, 'It shall be done!'

This pattern of constant prayer, night and day, was repeated at the 1905 convention, with Hyde frequently fasting throughout the day. Hardly surprisingly, revival came to Saikot, which had reverberations throughout India, including large numbers of conversions.

Absolute obedience

John Hyde's biographers are united in their view that prayer was *the* characteristic of his life and ministry. It gave his work a powerful unity and sense of purpose. His influence over other men was remarkable, not least because of his absolute obedience in prayer, ardent love for Jesus, a passionate regard for the men and women among whom he worked, and a genuine affection for his fellow missionaries. The essence of his life was summed up by McGaw like this:

> *It does not seem that John Hyde preached much about his own personal experiences of sanctification, but he lived the sanctified life. His life preached. Just as he did not say very much about prayer. He prayed. His life was a witness to the power of the blood of Jesus to cleanse from all sin.*

No more eloquent testimony is possible about a life wholly dedicated in service to God. Hyde's example, as well as his prayers that laid the basis for revival in India, still speak powerfully today. His humility resonates in this present age so flawed by the worship of men, the tendency to adopt the easy option, and the rank failure to spend time in prayer.

Hyde's life is both a rebuke and an encouragement to us all.

Challenge for today

Prayer was, quite simply, the *supreme activity* in John Hyde's all-too-brief life. It consumed him, whereas for most Christians it is a part-time occupation, exercised primarily in times of trouble and difficulty.

In addition, and closely related to his intense prayer life, Hyde lived a sanctified life that few of us approximate. God could see his seriousness

> Prayer was, quite simply, the *supreme activity* in John Hyde's all-too-brief life.

and, in His sovereign will, sent revival to India where, quite literally, Hyde burned himself out for God, dying well before the age of fifty. Today, God is looking for the same level of commitment and seriousness from us, but He wants to know whether we are similarly serious – or not. Only we, only *you*, know the answer to this.

Hyde did not allow himself to be sidetracked, either by the lethargy of others or by criticism – he simply pursued the pathway God had called him to. He kept on running the race.

Prayer

Father, we thank You for the remarkable legacy left by John Hyde. May it encourage and motivate us to pray for ourselves, our churches, our ministries and those members of our own families who do not, as yet, know You personally. Amen.

GEORGE JEFFREYS
(1889–1962)

Preacher and revivalist

George Jeffreys was born on 28 February 1889, in Maesteg, South Wales. Born into a large family in the Llynfi Valley, he had two brothers and nine sisters, including Stephen Jeffreys, dubbed by one critic as 'The Healing Evangelist'. The circumstances of his early life were, in reality, grim. His father, a coal miner, died aged forty-seven, while six of his brothers and sisters predeceased his mother Kezia, between the years 1879–1916. Poverty and unemployment were ever-present spectres as George grew up, facts he often alluded to later in life.

Converted and healed

George and Stephen were both converted during 1904 at a time when the conversions during the Welsh Revival totalled over 100,000. Little wonder that Lloyd George, the prime minister from 1916–22, likened the effect of the revival to a tornado, such was its cleansing, purifying and convicting power. Later, George Jeffreys, before entering his public ministry, was healed of a debilitating paralysis that seemed likely to prevent him becoming a minister. Gloriously set free in this way, he pursued an energetic, indeed exhausting, lifestyle for over forty years.

Called to preach

George Jeffreys' public ministry may be divided into two main phases. In 1915, he founded the Elim Pentecostal Movement, which had its roots in the re-discovery of the power of the Holy Spirit. For the next twenty-five years he gave himself unstintingly to the work of Elim, including his role as principal of the Bible College in Capel, near Dorking. Then, from 1940–62 (having withdrawn from Elim in 1940), he pursued an itinerant and international preaching ministry, quite literally throughout the world.

It is not an exaggeration to say that George Jeffreys was one of the greatest evangelists of the twentieth century, preaching to vast congregations both at home and abroad. One of the most significant meetings, conducted jointly by George and Stephen Jeffreys, took place in Hull in 1922, about which he wrote as follows:

> *What wonderful scenes were witnessed at the divine healing services. One woman told of nineteen long years of suffering through paralysis, but she was completely healed. Another lady related how after four years of suffering from hip disease, during which time she had undergone no less than four serious operations and had lain in irons for over three years, her case was pronounced as absolutely hopeless by the physicians. God stepped in and marvellously delivered her and now she is able to do her own housework.*

Another lady had not left her house for sixteen years, except in a bath-chair; three times she was operated upon. The doctors pronounced her case as incurable. She said she felt the power of God go through her from head to foot with a mighty thrill. Her bath-chair was dispensed with and, to the astonishment of her friends and neighbours, she walked home unaided. She testified: 'I have been able to do more housework these last eight weeks than I have done all my married life.'

Carrying on

Inevitably, George Jeffreys' departure from the Elim Movement in 1940 was a time of personal anguish for him. It did not, however, diminish his zeal for proclaiming the gospel, and he carried on doing that until his sudden death in 1962.

Throughout these years he remained the man of God he had always been. He was a man who loved the Word of God, seeing the Scriptures as the absolute authority in the Christian Church; a man of prayer; and a man of faith who once memorably told a minister who had asked him for advice: 'It is not your great faith that counts, but your little faith in a great God.'

> 'It is not your great faith that counts, but your little faith in a great God.'

Challenge for today

A product of the 1904–05 Welsh Revival, George Jeffreys returned to this fact time and time again in private conversation. Like Selwyn Hughes, it shaped his consciousness of what a classic revival looks like.

George Jeffreys was immensely serious about his Christian life, being particularly aware of the God-given authority Christians have in terms of healing the sick. Stupendous healings frequently accompanied his preaching. On one occasion, the first night of a campaign in Glasgow was very poorly attended, not in itself a fact that troubled him. At its conclusion, however, he walked off the platform, saw a woman in a wheelchair, and told her to get up in God's healing power. She did, and the next night the auditorium was crammed to capacity.

George Jeffreys' life challenges us to believe that God heals today. As Dr David Petts says in *Just a Taste of Heaven*: 'Jesus' commission to heal the sick was not limited to the period of Jesus' earthly ministry.' George Jeffreys believed that, but do we? Unpretentious in his demeanour, he was truly a man of God. What about us?

Prayer

Heavenly Father, You are the source of all good gifts, and we ask for the gift of faith to demonstrate Your kingdom in power today. But to do so we need a fresh impartation of Your dynamic Holy Spirit. We wait expectantly for such a filling. Amen.

STEPHEN JEFFREYS
(1876–1943)

Power evangelism

S tephen Jeffreys, in common with his brother George Jeffreys, was converted during the Welsh Revival of 1904–05. They were two of the 100,000 men and women ushered into the kingdom of God during a six-month period in 1904. They were also amongst the most influential of all the converts.

Into the mines

Born on 2 September 1876 into a poor family in Maesteg, South Wales, Stephen followed his father into the mines at the tender age of twelve, at a time when workers' rights were almost non-existent. Inevitably, life was extremely tough for him though he was blessed with a strong, even robust, physique that enabled him to cope more than adequately with the rigours of the mining industry where weakness – either physical or mental – was ruthlessly exposed and exploited.

From darkness to light

Before the revival, Stephen's interest in religion was, at best, nominal but he was totally unable to resist the power of the Holy Spirit and, on 17 November 1904, he was gloriously converted. Several years later he, again like George, experienced the baptism of the Holy Spirit.

Power evangelism

Thereafter Stephen Jeffreys' life was devoted – wholeheartedly and willingly – to the preaching of the gospel. He preached with enormous power, so much so that many of his services reproduced a number of the extraordinary features of Evan Roberts' revival. This is how one Sunday newspaper reported a series of meetings held in the tough colliery village of Aberaman, Aberdare, in 1919:

> Indeed, so remarkable are the scenes of intense religious fervour, coupled with supernatural visions on the part of converts and cases of what are claimed to be divine healing of physical diseases among them, that one aged religious leader declares that he has seen three revivals but that this is the greatest of them all!

In his preaching, the second coming of Christ featured prominently and, as Colin Whittaker says in *Seven Pentecostal Pioneers*, 'brought with it a great sense of urgency'.

Vast crowds were drawn to his meetings wherever he went, including extensive tours of America and Canada (in 1924) and Australia and New Zealand (in 1933).

Seemingly at the zenith of his powers, and not yet sixty, Stephen was struck down with arthritis and his last years were spent quietly in Wales. His wife, Elizabeth, died on 27 October 1943, and his own death followed soon after on 18 November 1943, exactly thirty-nine years after his dramatic conversion.

Reputation

Stephen and George Jeffreys were remarkable men from humble circumstances, but with a burning love for Jesus. Stephen was as flamboyant as George was dignified and sober. Stephen was pre-eminently an evangelist whereas George was both an evangelist and Bible teacher. Both led many thousands of people to faith in Jesus Christ and, rightly, enjoyed very considerable reputations.

Stephen Jeffreys was, in the considered judgment of the late Dr Martyn Lloyd-Jones, one of the greatest evangelists of the twentieth century. He was a man of energy and humility, whose sense of purpose and conviction in preaching the gospel remained steadfast for almost forty years. His whole thinking was governed by the teaching of the Bible, which he believed with a child-like simplicity.

His whole thinking was governed by the teaching of the Bible …

In addition, Stephen was a man who took prayer seriously, not as a duty but as a vital necessity for maintaining a living relationship with God. This spirit of prayer – allied to an unquenchable faith – sustained him during the long years of his illness and, as Colin Whittaker has wisely commented, 'His true worth was revealed in his uncomplaining and cheerful patience.' The conclusion seems inescapable: if revival is to break out and be sustained in Britain in the new millennium, leaders like Stephen Jeffreys will be required.

Challenge for today

As we have seen, Stephen Jeffreys was a product of the 1904–05 Welsh Revival and thereafter preached the gospel with vigour, total conviction and great power. He took the promises of God (in the Bible) with 'child-like simplicity' and faith – attitudes we, too, would do well to foster and maintain. People flocked to his meetings where they encountered not only anointed preaching, but also miracles of healing and restoration.

Born in humble and obscure circumstances, he exhibited the fruit of the Spirit (Gal. 5:22) in humility and graciousness, something that is required of all Christians.

Even though crippling illness and disability dogged his last years, Stephen Jeffreys remained cheerful to the end, being sustained by a caring wife and habits of faith that he had long cultivated in a public ministry of nearly forty years.

Prayer

Father in heaven, thank You for all the good times when we've been aware of Your many blessings. Remind us that Your grace is equally operative when we are going through times of adversity and sickness. Your grace is always sufficient, for which we are deeply grateful. Amen.

JOHN KILPATRICK
(born 1950)

Equipped to serve

John Kilpatrick is known throughout the Christian world as the senior pastor at Brownsville Assembly of God Church, Pensacola, where a revival was powerfully evident from 18 June 1995 (although it has since declined). At that time, Kilpatrick had been in full-time pastoral ministry for twenty-four years, so was hugely experienced in the running and organising of churches. Nothing, however, could have adequately prepared him for the descent of God's presence that great day – aptly, Father's Day. In fact, Kilpatrick had commented to the worship leader, Lindell Cooley, that 'Nothing happens on Father's Day', which was either an indication of a lack of faith or a realistic assessment of where his church stood at that particular moment. He was also grieving after the death of his beloved mother the previous month. But God did do something awesome, the effect of which has reverberated throughout the world.

Beginnings

An ordained minister with the Assemblies of God, John Kilpatrick was called to preach at the young age of fourteen in his home town in Georgia and, as he says in *Feast of Fire*, 'Nothing ever was going to change my mind.' Subsequently he attended Southwestern College, Florida and the Berean School of the Bible, Missouri, followed by a period pastoring two churches in Indiana and Florida.

1995: An explosion of the Spirit

It is difficult to escape the conclusion, though, that all these experiences, however valuable, were but the preparation for the main work of his life in Brownsville, Florida, where he was senior pastor for many years. Reading his autobiography *Feast of Fire*, it is clearly apparent that the years from 1991 are of crucial significance for understanding Kilpatrick's whole life and ministry. He felt God was calling him to build a house of power and a house of prayer where men and women from all denominations, backgrounds and circumstances could come and pray. He says:

> As the people began to pray, God would turn His house into a house of power where He could heal the sick and deliver the troubled in heart. That power would then quite naturally draw praise and thanksgiving from the people, making it now also a house of praise. That's when the children came around it crying 'Hosanna!'

So these four steps – purity, prayer, power and praise – are essential if we are going to see God's glory revealed.

These foundational emphases were then systematically taught to the church, not only by Kilpatrick himself but also by his friend, Dick Reuben, who perceptively said, 'When the pattern is right, God's glory falls.'

Personally, too, John Kilpatrick had to learn hard, though vitally important, lessons. Driving down the road one day God spoke to him directly and robustly, 'If you don't get rid of that critical spirit, I am going to pass you by.' His response, Renee De Loreia records in *Portals in Pensacola*, was 'immediate, he pulled the car over and repented'.

Changed perspectives

Inevitably, the aftermath of the mighty outpouring of June 1995 meant increased demands on his time and energies, with hungry people from all over the world coming to receive from God at the 'watering hole' that God established in Brownsville (though today this is far less intense than earlier). He was led to reach out to other pastors with a burden on his heart for the things that they experienced in the ministry, holding two Ministers' Conferences at Brownsville a year – not an instructional 'how-to', but rather a time set aside to love those in ministry and their families. He was also led to go out and speak at conferences, churches and civic arenas all across America, which God used as a tool to spread revival fire around the country. Kilpatrick's over-arching goal was to 'develop a ministry so thoroughly that it [would] effectively minister to everyone from the cradle to the grave'.

> So these four steps – purity, prayer, power and praise – are essential if we are going to see God's glory revealed.

Challenge for today

The dramatic revival broke out in Pensacola, Florida approximately eighteen months after the outbreak of the 'Toronto Blessing'. It affected many Pentecostal churches, but went on to have a worldwide impact. Key emphases of this move of God were holiness and the need to repent of spiritual compromise. Its human face, John Kilpatrick, along with his wife Brenda, had prayed for many long months for 'times of refreshing' in which God's glory would be demonstrated.

The challenge posed by Kilpatrick's experience is that we must rid ourselves of criticism of other Christians, and repent if we are guilty of any such behaviour. In other words, God is looking for cleansed vessels He can use in His service.

Sadly, the revival in Pensacola ended amidst recriminations between the leaders and, although they have been reconciled, their public falling-out left many people – including those who had been awoken from spiritual lethargy – bemused, even baffled. It is a stark warning that the most thrilling and reinvigorating of revivals can be brought to an end in disappointing and disheartening ways by the decisions and reactions of men and women.

Prayer

Father God, help us to accept other people, whatever their background, whatever their gifts. The unity of Your Church is of vital importance, so please give us the grace to preserve it at all costs. Amen.

DR MARTYN LLOYD-JONES
(1899–1981)

Longing for revival

D r Martyn Lloyd-Jones held two pastorates in a preaching ministry of over fifty years. The first, in Aberavon, South Wales (1927–38) followed his decision to leave a potentially lucrative career in medicine. The second, at Westminster Chapel, London from 1938–68, saw his emergence as one of the most influential evangelicals in Britain in the second half of the twentieth century. He brought to both churches outstanding pastoral and preaching gifts, and two of his greatest series of sermons at Westminster on Romans and Ephesians continue to influence people throughout the world in print and on tape.

During the long and successful years of his ministry, few subjects exercised his attention more consistently and rigorously than prayer, evangelism and revival. His views on all three were typically trenchant, robust, always biblically based, and unfailingly presented with balance and care. His views were also deeply informed by his acute theological understanding and his voracious reading of history, especially church history.

Longing for revival

This profile concerns Dr Lloyd-Jones's views on revival. He wrote: 'I long for revival comparable to that of the eighteenth century. More and more I am convinced that there, and there alone, lies our hope' (letter dated 13 March 1945). Not only did he long for revival, he prayed for it daily (his word) and exhorted his congregations to do the same. The same unshakeable conviction is expressed in a letter seventeen years later: 'The great need is for strong preaching which convicts through the power of the Holy Spirit', which he saw supremely demonstrated in the events of Pentecost.

Distinctive teaching

What then were the distinctives of Dr Martyn Lloyd-Jones's teaching on revival? He saw revival as:

- *Vital for the world as a whole.* Because he believed that the most important thing for the world is a strong vibrant Church, it follows that a revived, purified Church is the best of all as it affects society radically, inculcating a fresh sense of God and a heightened morality in general.
- *Entirely the work and activity of the Holy Spirit*, which no technique or strategy can produce. As he said, 'If you believe in the sovereignty of God, you must believe that whatever the state of the church, God can send revival', and 'Revival is something wrought by God in sovereign freedom, often in spite of men'.
- *Possible to be prepared for.* This emphasis does not, in his view, contradict the concept of the sovereignty of God because he saw preparation (he called them 'preliminaries') as an indication to God that men and women are serious about revival, serious about the things of God *in general* and, therefore, exactly the type of people whom God can bless with His purging fire of revival. There were three aspects to this preparation: *praying* intensely on a daily basis, *preaching* the Word of God, especially the cardinal and fundamental articles of the Christian faith, including God's nature as the sovereign, transcendent living God who acts, and *thirsting* for God.

- *A repetition of what happened at Pentecost.* In *The Puritans*, he puts it like this:

Revival is an outpouring of the Spirit of God. It is a kind of repetition of Pentecost. It is the Spirit descending upon people. This needs to be emphasized in this present age. For we have been told so much recently by some that every man at regeneration receives the baptism of the Spirit, and all he has to do after that is to surrender to what he has already. But revival does not come as a result of a man surrendering to what he already has; it is the Spirit being poured out upon him, descending upon him, as happened on the day of Pentecost.

- *A visitation.* In *Revival* he defines its essence as 'the Holy Spirit coming down' corporately and individually, even nationally. The theme of God's outpouring of His Holy Spirit was something he returned to again and again in his preaching.
- *Distinct from renewal.* In a lecture on Jonathan Edwards, he says this:

Today, we are hearing much about what is called 'renewal'. They dislike the term revival; they prefer 'renewal'. What they mean by that is that we have all been baptized with the Spirit at the moment of regeneration, and that all we have to do therefore is to realize what we already have and yield ourselves to it. That is not revival! You can do all they teach and derive many benefits; but you still have not had revival. Revival is an out-pouring of the Spirit. It is something that comes upon us, that happens to us.

… he brought all his gifts under the authority and discipline of God's Word.

- *The only hope.* In a letter dated 3 March 1942, he writes:

The only hope, I see more and more clearly, is a revival. I feel we are called to pray for such a movement. Nothing else can deal with the terrible state of the country, and of the world. In any case our business is to sow the seed in hope, knowing that God alone can give the increase.

Aberavon 1927–38

Poignantly, he was never part of a national revival, though his biographer Iain Murray refers to some of the events at Aberavon (1927–38) as a revival. In particular, he refers to the period 1930–31, when the church there experienced particularly powerful demonstrations of the Holy Spirit in terms of frequent and remarkable conversions. Significantly though, Lloyd-Jones himself never once referred to these events at Aberavon in terms of revival, but he continued to pray for an outpouring of the Holy Spirit right up to his death. As he said, 'What is needed is not a stunt but the *action of God* that will stun people.' That is as valid today as it was when his earthly ministry closed on 1 March 1981.

Challenge for today

Widely recognised as one of the greatest evangelical preachers of the twentieth century, the challenge for us from Lloyd-Jones's life is to go on preaching the Word of God consistently and to pray for revival unceasingly even if revival does not come.

To hear 'the Doctor' (as he was invariably known) preaching was a thrilling experience, and his sermons are readily available as tapes and books. They preserve his manifest delight in proclaiming 'justification by faith' as the only means for men and women to move 'out of darkness into [God's] wonderful light' (1 Pet. 2:9).

Dr Lloyd-Jones was a brilliant man intellectually, but he brought all his gifts under the authority and discipline of God's Word.

Prayer

O God, help us to pray unceasingly for a fresh outpouring of Your Spirit. Guard our hearts against any form of disappointment or disillusionment if it does not happen. Strengthen us to go on in faith and in the confidence that comes from You. Amen.

DAVID MORGAN (1814–83) and HUMPHREY JONES (1832–95)

The greatness of two ordinary men

The most dominating name in the history of revival in Wales is, of course, Evan Roberts. This fact tends to obscure the work and influence of these two men of God. This is a pity because they were powerfully – though not exclusively in the same sense as Roberts – used by God in the 1859 revival that swept through Wales with such significant effect.

Backgrounds

David Morgan was born, in 1814, into an extremely large family – he was the third of nine children – that eventually settled in Ysbyty Ystwyth, Cardiganshire. He worked as a carpenter under the guidance of his father, but from 1842 he devoted his life to preaching the gospel, eventually becoming a minister with the Calvinistic Methodists in May 1857.

Humphrey Jones's background was equally humble and unpretentious. He started preaching with the Wesleyan Methodists but was rejected from the ministry and subsequently spent several years in America where he became an ordained minister with the Methodist Episcopal Church.

An important alliance

The year 1858 was crucial for Jones, for two reasons. First, he returned to Wales and, second, he encountered David Morgan who, in Colin Whittaker's words, was

> somewhat sceptical, but on hearing young Jones preach he was greatly moved and within a few days [Morgan himself] was preaching under a new anointing from God. His own village had only a population of a thousand but before the end of the year 200 converts had been won.

A year later, in 1859, revival swept through Wales, but also through England, Ireland and Scotland. During 1859–60, the revival permeated throughout the whole of Wales, with Morgan preaching about four times each day. There was an intensity and a conviction about the meetings and here is David Morgan's son's description of the outbreak of revival in a Carmarthenshire town:

> One Sunday morning an elder rose to speak and his first remark was that the God they worshipped was without beginning and without end. 'Amen!' exclaimed a young girl in the highest notes of a lovely voice, 'Blessed be His name forever!' This cry might be compared to the touch of the electric button that shivers a quarry into a thousand hurtling fragments. Scores leaped from their seats, and, gathering in the vacant space in the centre, they gave vent to their pent-up emotion in outcries that were almost agonising in their ardour and intensity.

Lasting fruit

Under the leadership of David Morgan, Humphrey Jones and others, the effects of the 1859 revival were both striking and significant. It is interesting to note three important effects. First, all sections of society were affected, from intellectual students to the roughest of quarry men and miners. Second, it is estimated that 100,000 people were added to the Church, and this out of a total population of 1 million. Third, crime was drastically reduced, the Welsh Courts reporting in 1860 a decrease from 1,809 to 1,228 cases.

Aftermath

The 1859 revival was, without doubt, the high point in the public ministries of both David Morgan and Humphrey Jones. Following a period of physical and mental ill health, Jones and his family left for America in 1871, where he died in Wisconsin on 8 May 1895. There's little doubt that, like Evan Roberts later on, he was physically exhausted by the revival and was never the same man again. Morgan, after the heat of revival had declined, returned to conventionally routine Church life. He died on 27 October 1883. The 'ordinariness' of their lives after the revival does not detract at all from their qualities as men of God (prayerful, humble and obedient), their significance, or their formative influence on the Welsh Revival of 1859. They were simple country ministers who were given a vision by God and did their upmost to fulfil it. Their faithfulness is worth recalling in an age of doubt and cynicism.

> The 'ordinariness' of their lives after the revival does not detract at all from their qualities as men of God ...

Challenge for today

Both Morgan and Jones were ordinary men whose ministries were powerfully impacted by the 1859 revival in Wales. In fact, after hearing Humphrey Jones preach one night, Morgan was profoundly affected by the message, saying later: 'I went to bed that night just David Morgan as usual, I awoke the next morning feeling like a lion, feeling that I was filled with the power of the Holy Ghost.' The results of this baptism of the Holy Spirit were quite simply tremendous: large numbers were converted and added to the Church, and society was pervaded by a rejoicing in the things of God. One such person to be affected by Morgan's newfound power in preaching was Thomas Charles

Edwards who later became the first principal of the University of Wales, Aberystwyth and, eventually, the president of the first theological college of the Calvinistic Methodist Church.

Like Paul in Acts 16:9–10, both Morgan and Jones were prayerful, humble, obedient and faithful to the 'heavenly vision' God had imparted to them. The challenge for us is whether we are similarly open to the promptings of the Holy Spirit.

Prayer

Father God, we ask You to keep on speaking to us through Your Spirit, even when our ears are apparently closed. We ask Your forgiveness for not listening to Your Word, and that we might be faithful to Your guidance. Amen.

ROBERT MURRAY McCHEYNE

(1813–43)

Holy man of God

'Men whom God uses in revival have always been men who maintained a close walk with God and longed for a holy life.' Robert Murray McCheyne was such a man. His perpetual prayer, 'Lord, make me and my ministers as holy as a saved sinner can be' captures not only his sincerity but also his willingness to surrender fully to the Person and claims of Christ. He is one of those men whose abiding influence has nothing to do with the length of his life – he died, after all, at the age of twenty-nine.

Revival in Dundee

Educated at Edinburgh University, the death of his elder brother caused him to reflect seriously on his own spiritual condition, the upshot being a radical conversion and then, becoming a Church of Scotland minister. In 1836, he took charge of St Peter's Church, Dundee, where he devoted himself to direct and passionate preaching of the gospel. Three years later, writing of the revival in Dundee, he commented:

The ministers have preached, so far as I can judge, nothing but the Gospel of the grace of God. They have done this fully, clearly, solemnly; with discrimination, urgency and affection. None of them read their sermons. They all, I think, seek the immediate conversion of people, and they believe that, under a living gospel ministry, success is more or less the rule, and want of success the exception.

Another contributory reason to the revival in Dundee was the dedicated prayer lives of the people of that town. As McCheyne said himself:

I found thirty-nine such meetings held recently in connection with the congregation, and five of these were conducted and attended entirely by little children. At present [March 1841, two years after the beginning of the revival] … I believe the number of these meetings is not much diminished.

But there was also opposition to this vibrant life of God, and Brian Edwards helpfully comments in his book on revival, 'Opposition to the gospel will be greater in the time of revival. Normally the world can ignore the Church, but when revival comes it cannot.' How true these words are of McCheyne's experiences in Dundee when, as he said himself, 'The effects that have been produced upon the community are very marked, including a greater awareness of the importance of the Sabbath.' Hundreds of men and women continued to live in abject sin and misery, of course, but even they could not deny that God was at work powerfully in their community.

Godly radiance

This profound seriousness was something the people observed in McCheyne himself, whose entry into the pulpit was sufficient to cause mature Christians to weep. There was a solemnity about him which, according to Dr Martyn Lloyd-Jones, had a particular source: 'He had come from the presence of God … There was a radiance of God about him.' The fruitfulness of McCheyne's ministry was the outcome of two factors. One was his strict daily programme of Bible study, prayer and meditation. Another was his consuming passion for God which is encapsulated in a story told after his death. It is recorded that a young man, seeking the reasons for the success of McCheyne's ministry, was taken into his study by an old man who instructed him as follows: 'Sit down and weep – that's what McCheyne used to do before he preached.'

In retrospect

In spite of his early death, McCheyne's influence on Scotland was profound and long-lasting. Not because of the institutions he founded or the works of theology he wrote, but because of his consistent example of holy living, transparent honesty and the desire to please God with every fibre of his being. His life is a sharp rebuke to the sort of easy believism and arrogance that masquerades for Christian life and holiness today. How good it is, therefore, that his influence extended far beyond the confines of Scotland with the publication in 1862 of Andrew Bonar's book, *Memoirs and Remains of Robert McCheyne*. Ultimately, his life shows that there is no simple route to revival.

'Lord, make me and my ministers as holy as a saved sinner can be' ...

Challenge for today

Robert Murray McCheyne's influence within evangelicalism is in inverse proportion to the brevity of his life. He died suddenly and unexpectedly aged twenty-nine, but his name lives on as a shining example for us today: first, of how to conduct and pastor a revival by remaining true to God's Word; second, as a man of integrity, holiness and gracious Christian behaviour. There was a godly radiance about him that was immensely attractive to Christians and non-Christians alike.

Murray McCheyne was a man of action, not merely words. He did not talk about prayer – he prayed. And he did not talk about being holy – he lived a holy life. Andrew Bonar said: 'The real secret of his soul's prosperity lay in daily enlargement of his heart in fellowship with God.' As Murray McCheyne said in his diary, 'I ought to spend the best hours of the day in communion with God.' But lest it be thought that his was a gloomy, negative sort of holiness, it needs to be emphasised that as a person he was warm-hearted and humorous. He remains an example to be emulated by us all.

Prayer

O God, our hearts' desire is to be holy, but we fear that we lack the resolve and the determination. Ravage our hearts again with Your love, so that we may love You and be compassionate to others. Amen.

JOHN NEWTON
(1725–1807)

Revivalist and letter-writer

To set the scene

The eighteenth-century Methodist Revival, also known as the Evangelical Awakening it prompted, was led initially by such people as John Wesley, his brother Charles, George Whitefield and Daniel Rowland, but as the revival spread, other leaders came into prominence, including John Newton. Formerly a slave captain, he was dramatically converted, an experience alluded to in his hymns 'Glorious Things of Thee are Spoken', 'Amazing Grace' and 'How Sweet the Name of Jesus Sounds'. A remarkable feature of the people referred to immediately above was their diversity of gifts. John Wesley led the attack, an inspirer and organiser of genius; his brother Charles wrote hymns which have become a permanent part of the evangelical heritage; Whitefield was a truly great preacher; and Newton was peculiarly equipped to deal with individual souls, declaring that his 'favourite branch' of the divine truth was 'the human heart with its workings and counter-workings'. Newton's special and distinctive contribution to the Evangelical Revival was as a letter-writer par excellence.

The characteristic features of Newton's letters

To read Newton's pastoral letters is to be acutely conscious of a large and generous heart in a century noted for its heartlessness and inhumanity; and secondly, it is to sense the nerve centre, the pulse, of a transforming and ennobling faith, a saving faith that was 'a disposition of the heart'.

Three features of Newton's faith may be highlighted. It was:

- *Firmly and uncompromisingly Christo-centric.* He stresses repeatedly that by nature 'we are strangers, yea, enemies to God; but we are reconciled, brought nigh, and become His children, by faith in Christ Jesus'. He defines the Christian as a 'new creature, born and taught from above'; and as someone 'once convinced of his guilt and misery as a sinner, has fled for refuge to the hope set before him, has seen the Son and believed in Him'. As such, those who are 'born from above' are 'united to Jesus, they are delivered from condemnation, and are heirs of eternal life, and may therefore well be accounted happy'. To Newton, the only way for a person to enjoy peace was an absolute commitment to Jesus Christ: 'By casting our burdens upon Him, our spirits become light and cheerful; we are freed from a thousand anxieties and inquietudes which are wearisome to our minds, and which with respect to events, are needless for us, yea, useless.'
- *Based upon knowledge.* Over and over again, Newton refers in his letters to the nature and function of God's Word. For example, in a letter discussing the relationship between the enlightening of a person's understanding and the Scriptures, he says:

Now as God only thus reveals Himself by the medium of Scripture truth, the light received this way leads the soul to the Scripture from whence it springs, and all the leading truths of the Word of God soon begin to be perceived and assented to.

- *Meditative and practical.* So much Christianity today is like our consumer-conscious, mass-media world in which the superficial, the glib and the flashy are all important: the image is so often mistaken for the reality. Not so Newton who was concerned with 'soul exercises' – to him, the Christian life begins with a clear understanding of the gospel which a non-believer does not have. It is an inner life in which 'the very desire and bent of the soul is to God, and to the Word of His grace', a life in which a person's desires are fixed 'supremely upon Jesus Christ'. This life also expresses itself in humility, in submission to the will of God, in a longing for progress in the life of holiness. Communion with God is a daily aspect, while every avenue of life is permeated by the love of God.

Newton's letters are glowingly alive – as are his hymns – with a warm, passionate, confident faith, which emanated from an experience of the gospel which was both personal and triumphant.

Challenge for today

Newton's conversion was dramatic and comprehensive: truly an illustration of God's amazing grace. Thereafter he delighted in the 'name of Jesus'. Newton was a vital component in the Methodist Revival, or Evangelical Awakening, as a 'letter-writer', giving individuals sensitive, biblical and encouraging advice.

The challenge of John Newton's life is found in the way he allowed the Holy Spirit to transform him from rough slave trader to supportive counsellor. Selwyn Hughes once said that 'good counselling methodology arises from good theology', which was certainly the case with Newton.

> Christian life begins with a clear understanding of the gospel ...

Prayer

Lord, give us the desire to serve You wholeheartedly by serving our fellow men and women in love and acceptance. Warm our hearts and emotions so that we can empathise with others. Amen.

JESSIE PENN-LEWIS
(1861–1927)

Prayer warrior

Jessie Penn-Lewis was an extraordinary woman whose life has attracted admiration and criticism in almost equal proportions. With the benefit of history, however, few balanced and judicious critics would deny that her achievements were quite outstanding; and this despite the burden of extremely fragile health. Frequently in serious physical weakness, she nevertheless travelled extensively at home and abroad, visiting such countries as America, Canada, Egypt, Russia and Scandinavia to address public conferences and private audiences.

Dedicated to God

Such a lifestyle was a far cry from the South Wales mining village, Neath, where she was born on 28 July 1861. Her childhood memories, as she herself recorded, were 'gathered around the great gathering of the Sunday School on the first Sunday in May and the coming to and fro of ministers. I was therefore brought up in the lap of Calvinist Methodism.' Taught to read from the Bible at the age of four, and in a family who delighted in books, her conversion occurred on 1 January 1882, two years after her marriage to William Penn-Lewis. She wrote:

> I used to take down my Bible from the shelf and read it occasionally. I turned
> over a page and my eye fell on the words, 'The Lord laid on Him the iniquity
> of us all'. By chance I turned the pages of the Holy Book and saw these
> words, 'He who believes hath eternal life'. After a few minutes of musing I saw
> that it was saying truly that I had everlasting life if I would believe simply on
> the Word. Then there was a sudden cry – I Do Believe, and my soul was filled
> with deep peace.

Thereafter her life was dedicated to serving God, to obeying Him whatever the cost to herself. This emphasis became the central message of her speaking and writing for the next thirty-five years.

Fullness of joy

A significant year in Jessie's life was 1889. On 21–22 February she was baptised in the Holy Spirit. This experience prepared her for one of the most important roles of her life: interpreting the Welsh Revival 1904–05 for a global audience, most notably as a special correspondent for Wales, and as a feature writer for *The Christian*. In these writings she was emphatic that the revival had its source in worldwide 'chains of prayer'. To Jessie, the great outpourings of prayer in the revival were its 'hidden springs of power and holiness'; and she was equally convinced that it was prayer that sustained the spiritual effect of the revival for many years afterwards. Girded by prayer too, she was instrumental in the recovery of Evan Roberts who had been spiritually, emotionally and physically exhausted by the many demands of the 1904–05 Welsh Revival.

An appraisal

For over thirty years, Jessie Penn-Lewis's life was extremely busy, even hectic, during all of which time she was faithfully and loyally supported by her husband, William. Her contribution to Christian thought and piety was considerable, as her most recent biographer, Brynmor Pierce Jones, shows in *The Trials and Triumphs of Jessie Penn-Lewis*. He identifies four primary aspects of this contribution:

- An extended interpretation of spiritual warfare to include not only cosmic conflict and social disorders but that hidden inner conflict within the soul whenever oppressed and harassed by deceptions, counterfeits and sudden despairs and doubts.
- The deep teaching about prayer and intercession and its relationship to spiritual warfare.
- The crystal clear teaching about the principles of Christian living summed up in two books, *Soul and Spirit* and *Four Planes of Spiritual Life*.
- The comprehensive presentation of every possible outworking of the cross of Christ in both cosmos and community, Church life and individual life. How the cross affected Satan, sin and death, and how it related to our salvation.

> Jessie Penn-Lewis challenges us today to be people of faith, prayer, worship and deep devotion to the Lord Jesus.

Her last essays have the title 'These All Died in Faith'; Jessie herself did during August 1927. To the very end, she gloried in the cross of Jesus, prayed unceasingly, and left an example of overcoming faith for future generations.

Challenge for today

'Remarkable' is an overused word today in the secular and Christian worlds, but it is entirely appropriate when applied to Jessie Penn-Lewis, whose life was a patchwork of trials and triumphs.

She overcame the Victorian restrictions and prejudices faced by women, virulent personal criticism and considerable ill-health, to spend the last thirty years of her life in extremely busy, indeed frenetic, Christian ministry. She wrote fifty books or booklets on key aspects of the Christian faith, their central message being 'to obey the will of God whenever and wherever He calls, to perceive the Holy Spirit's manifold ministries, to fully trust in Christ crucified and exalted, and to be delivered from all doubts, deceits, and dangers'.

Jessie Penn-Lewis challenges us today to be people of faith, prayer, worship and deep devotion to the Lord Jesus.

Prayer

Heavenly Father, we often lack faith in You and Your ways, so we beseech You once again for the reinvigoration that comes from the effusion of the Holy Spirit. We long to live in the fullness of the life that only You can give. Amen.

EVAN ROBERTS
(1878–1951)

Fit for the Master's use

Evan Roberts was at the nerve centre of the Welsh Revival of
1904–05. Its human face or, as he put it, 'one agent', his name
reverberated throughout Wales and the world between November
1904 and August 1905. As with the leaders of the 'Toronto Blessing'
ninety years later, he faced fierce and unrelenting criticism, because
of the emotional scenes and manifestations, to which he replied
adamantly:

> *God's Spirit came to me one night, when upon my knees I
> asked Him for guidance, and five months later I was baptised
> with the Spirit. I know that the work which has been done
> through me is not due to any human ability that I possess. It
> is His work and to His glory.*

For Roberts it was infinitely more important to follow God's guidance
than to respond to human wisdom and direction.

Family background

A native of Loughor, South Wales, Evan Roberts was the ninth child of fourteen children born to Henry and Hannah Roberts. His father was a coal miner and, by the age of twelve, Evan was accompanying his father to the coal face, an occupation requiring considerable reserves of determination and courage. Leaving school so early meant that his education, at least in conventional terms, was partial and inadequate.

Chosen by God

Looking back from the twenty-first century, the temptation might be to see the choice of Evan Roberts as God's instrument in one of the greatest supernatural moves in Church history as surprising, even inappropriate. Of limited experience, possessing a sensitive and reserved personality, he was not a particularly gifted individual. This was not surprising given the poverty of his home and the premature end to his childhood when he followed his father into the rough and tumble world of mining.

Levels of character

What may not have been apparent to human beings, however, was crystal clear to God, because Evan Roberts had built into his life traits of character and faith that God could use to accomplish His purposes. Five key factors, in particular, are worth recalling.

- *Remarkable standards as a young man.* He was, in the eyes of his fellow miners (always the most robust critics of their fellow men and sharply alert to the bogus and the hypocritical), a 'good worker', prepared to work hard to master the tasks allocated to him. He developed habits of discipline that he needed in abundance later on.
- *Intensity of his spiritual experience.* He took God and His demands seriously, and he valued the direction and advice of those in spiritual authority over him. Brynmor Pierce Jones records an occasion when

a godly deacon exhorted people to come to the means of grace more regularly. He reminded them that when Thomas was absent from the upper room, he had missed that vital moment when the Lord came and breathed His Spirit into the others. At once the impressionable young lad vowed that he would never be absent from such meeting and that he would also wait and pray faithfully for the coming of the Holy Spirit. (An Instrument of Revival, p.5)

- *Devoted prayer life.* For eleven years (before 1904), Evan Roberts prayed and interceded passionately for an outpouring of the Holy Spirit. He frequently prayed through the night (a practice that caused his friends great concern) imploring God to visit Wales in revival power.

> He frequently prayed through the night ...

- *Obedience to God's voice.* By 1902, he was clearly aware of God's call to preach the gospel to the unconverted, a task he viewed as a 'privilege' (his word), and so he left the mining industry to prepare himself for the work ahead. He also resolutely turned his back on all desires to be a poet, a vocation highly respected in Wales then as today.
- *Acute understanding of the Holy Spirit's work.* He wrote:

The baptism of the Holy Spirit is the essence of revival, for revival comes from a knowledge of the Holy Spirit and the way of co-working with Him which enables Him to work in revival power. The primary condition of revival is therefore that believers should individually know the baptism of the Holy Spirit.

Out of this understanding grew his repeated emphasis on the outpouring of the Holy Spirit; and he taught that such an event was governed by four conditions:

1. *Confession of all past sins;*
2. *Searching out of all secret and doubtful things;*
3. *Obedience to the Holy Spirit, full and without reserve;* and
4. *Public declaration of Jesus Christ as Saviour.*

So while Evan Roberts was being prepared for the supreme work of his life, Wales too was undergoing a preparation and, by 1904, there was an awareness in many parts of the Principality that revival was about to break out. It did, too, at the end of October (1904) and the rest, as they say, is history.

Looking back

Many years have elapsed since those tumultuous days. They have not dimmed, however, the interest in Evan Roberts. The various accounts of his life are united in stressing his seriousness, prayerfulness, obedience to the Holy Spirit's guidance and his passionate desire to see God's will prevail in Wales and worldwide. He truly was a man of God whose cry of 'Bend the church and save the world' is still relevant and resonates powerfully in the hearts of all those interested in revival today.

Challenge for today

The key to the whole of Roberts' life was his consistent, dedicated prayer life before, during and after revival. Once convinced of Wales' need for revival, he prayed unceasingly for over eleven years for an outpouring of the Holy Spirit. Once revival fell in 1904 he determined to follow the Spirit's promptings whatever the cost; and he did so even in the face of strident, unrelenting criticism. Though gentle and unassertive by nature, his answer to the critics was resolute:

> Some things have been said about meetings, and about me, which are not true; but God's truth has not been hurt by these mis-statements and they, therefore, matter little. The power of revival in South Wales is not of men, but of God.

Prayer

O Father, help us to be prayerful and obedient men and women. And, like Roberts, to be obedient to your voice and guidance. Give us the grace to face opposition and to answer criticism with the dignity and wisdom that comes from You. Amen.

AIMEE SEMPLE McPHERSON
(1890–1944)

A woman who cared

Aimee Semple McPherson will undoubtedly be remembered as one of the greatest women evangelists of the twentieth century, as well as one of the most colourful and dynamic. She founded the International Church of the Foursquare Gospel, which, by the time of her death in 1944, had 400 branch churches. She was also the first woman to be granted a licence to operate a radio station, and programmes from the Angelus Temple (founded in 1923) reached thousands of men and women with the gospel. She was quite simply known as 'The Mother of Christian Radio in America'. Strikingly beautiful, she had a flair for the dramatic and her meetings, with their well-known emphasis on divine healing, drew vast crowds to the 5,300-seater Angelus Temple.

Humble beginnings

Such fame, publicity and, without doubt, controversy, was a far cry from her early days. She was born Aimee Elizabeth Kennedy on a small, indeed obscure, farm near Ingersoll, Ontario, Canada. She came to a personal knowledge of sins forgiven at the age of seventeen through the preaching of Robert Semple, whom she subsequently married, after which they set about pioneering evangelism in Canada and America.

Tragedy

Robert and Aimee then travelled to Hong Kong, with a determination to serve as 'faith missionaries' in China, but within a few weeks Robert had died of malaria, leaving her, at the tender age of twenty, a widow with a baby. In New York, having recovered from the after-effects of this tragedy, Aimee married an aspiring businessman named Harold McPherson, a marriage that was doomed to failure. Why? One of her biographers, explaining the breakdown in their relationship, said that Harold acted as the 'advance man', with Aimee following him up with her preaching. She had a striking presence, wonderful communication powers and an emphasis on healing, and this attracted the crowds. She launched the monthly magazine *The Bridal Call* in 1917, and wrote articles expounding the essence of her teaching. Unfortunately, Aimee's success strained her marriage beyond redemption and the couple were divorced in 1921.

Pressing on

Personal problems, however, did not diminish her dedication to the gospel and, blessed with stunning pulpit oratory, she brought countless thousands of people under the sound of Jesus' saving grace. But it wasn't only in the pulpit she showed her passion for soul-winning – she went to clubs, theatres, jails, dance halls and even brothels. As someone said at that time, 'There was no pleading, no fire and brimstone, no criticising, just a warm-hearted welcome from a woman who cared.'

And press on she did, despite being the subject of ferocious criticism, a mysterious disappearance when she was kidnapped in Mexico in 1926, and a disastrous marriage to David L. Hutton in 1931. Perhaps her resilience and courage is best illustrated by referring to the fact that during the Depression in the 1930s, she met the physical needs of 1.5 million people; a staggering feat. Her compassion for the needy was legendary. One reporter saw her feeding, encouraging, giving hope, faith and strength to the poor; in her home, there were sick women on the floor and elderly men in her garage.

The legacy

Aimee Semple McPherson's life was devoted to bringing the gospel to ordinary men and women – she was, in a phrase she herself liked, 'Everybody's Sister'. She died at the comparatively young age of fifty-three, but the denomination she founded lives on, with over 27,000 churches in over 100 countries of the world. Truly, she was a remarkable woman.

Challenge for today

Aimee Semple McPherson was a determined and brave woman. She had to endure a number of sad events, including the premature death of her first husband and the breakdown of her second and third marriages, but throughout all of these dispiriting events she remained vigorous in her faith and courage. She challenges us to face our difficulties with a similarly robust attitude.

Aimee Semple McPherson was a dedicated preacher of the gospel. She also had huge compassion for the poor, the needy, the dispossessed, the sick and the dysfunctional. Her life of loving, caring acts embodied what she taught and preached, and so challenges those who see preaching as an end in itself. Her faith gave her strength and the resolve to rise above complex personal problems and unpleasant and deeply hurtful criticism in a constructive and resilient way, an example that impressed the many thousands of people who came under her influence.

> Her compassion for the needy was legendary.

Prayer

O God, give us eyes to discern those who are needy and also the desire to help them in practical and loving ways. We need Your strength to be Your hands in a troubled and torn world. Amen.

CHARLES HADDON SPURGEON
(1834–92)

The preacher

Charles Haddon Spurgeon became the pastor of the Baptist church in the village of Waterbeach at the tender age of seventeen. Two years later he arrived in London to pastor the New Park Street Chapel. The novelty of the 'boy preacher' attracted novelty seekers, scoffers and the curious. And yet, as we read those sermons today, we see that while Spurgeon was a man of his time, his life and ministry *transcended* time, place and fashion.

His was a soul suffused with the grace of God. As hundreds who had come with shabby motives were brought under the conviction of sin, this led to a profound repentance, and finally moved into salvation. Spurgeon resisted the temptations of spectacular success with unfailing humility, and the personal certainty of his utter dependence on God.

Whatever preparations he made before preaching, they always included earnest and fervent prayer, and prayer for the presence and activity of the Holy Spirit. Here was a man of great gifts and formidable energy.

He had a powerful intelligence supplied from a vast and tenacious memory, and exceptional oratorical skills aided by a powerful and melodious voice, but all were surrendered to God, and sustained by constant prayer. God's impact on Victorian England through this one man was remarkable, with thousands upon thousands entering the kingdom, new churches opening supplied with pastors trained in a new college, schools, an orphanage ... the list goes on and on. This was a ministry bringing the reviving gift of repentance to all manner and conditions of humanity.

Not surprisingly, Spurgeon faced opposition, too. He was vilified in the press, and even in some pulpits. But, with a congregation that had grown from around eighty to over six thousand in just six years, a new building, The Metropolitan Tabernacle, was commissioned to accommodate them all.

The leader

As a leader, Spurgeon saw Christ's leadership example with great clarity, through eyes unclouded by selfish ambition, through a house clean of pride and, in the light of this knowledge, worked mightily to honour all believers as ministers and servants of the Lord Jesus Christ. The result was that he equipped thousands of men and women for the work of the kingdom, a task he tackled with incredible energy and supernatural wisdom. While we have available to us a vast treasure house of his sermons, he asked that his pulpit prayers should not be copied down. One exception was his prayer at the watch-night service of 1856, which was recorded. A brief passage from it reveals his conviction that revival is God's sovereign work:

Come Holy Spirit, we can do nothing without Thee. We solemnly invoke Thee, great Spirit of God! Thou who didst rest on Abraham, on Isaac and on Jacob; Thou who in the night visions speaketh unto men. Spirit of the Prophets, Spirit of the Apostles, Spirit of the Church, be Thou our Spirit this night, that the earth may tremble, that souls may be made to hear Thy word, and that all flesh may rejoice together to praise Thy name, Son and Holy Ghost, the dread Supreme, be everlasting praise. Amen.

Motivated by love

Charles Haddon Spurgeon was a gentle, sensitive man, easily moved to tears, a man willing to share the distress of those he encountered and be sympathetic with their infirmities. And he was a man ever ready to respond with joy and laughter. Through all the awesome work and mighty achievements that God accomplished through Spurgeon, one supreme gift, the gift of love, shines through it all; a love shed abroad in his heart in great abundance, a love that led thousands upon thousands to God. This love enabled him to tread an uncompromising path through the snares of extravagant praise and shocking abuse.

> His life challenges us to reflect on how we treat other people ...

Challenge for today

Spurgeon was a talented and able individual with an acute intelligence who brought to his preaching supreme skills as an orator. But he was impressive too in purely human terms: he was able, in particular, to empathise with all sorts of people, whatever their problems and whatever their status in life.

Above all, he was noted for his love that had its wellspring in the love he had received from Jesus. His life challenges us to reflect on how we treat other people, perhaps especially those who disagree with us or with whom we disagree. In this context, read John 13, a narrative in which Jesus showed His disciples 'the full extent of his love' (v.1). Jesus was pre-eminently a servant (Mark 10:45), something Spurgeon learned early in his preaching ministry. How do we see ourselves in God's kingdom? Is it with pride, or a sense of superiority? Neither attitude is appropriate, as Spurgeon's life showed.

Prayer

Heavenly Father, we often find it far from easy to love others, so we need Your help. We also need a fresh impartation of the love so wonderfully demonstrated by Your Son. Amen.

CHARLES WESLEY
(1707–88)

Hymn-writer and revivalist

Charles and John. Or John and Charles. The order in which their names are listed is largely irrelevant because theirs was a *life-long relationship* in many significant ways.

Both Charles and John Wesley were heavily influenced by their dominating – even intimidating – mother; both were educated at Oxford where the 'Holy Club' was such an important part of their lives; both received assurance of their salvation in 1738 (Charles on 21 May and John on 24 May); both were brought up as Anglicans; both were revivalists; both were influential in establishing Methodism as a powerful religious and social force in eighteenth-century Britain; and even today, though much weaker than it once was, the Methodist Church has a worldwide membership of approximately 24 million people.

Dramatic change

It is appropriate therefore to link these two gifted men, the significance of whose conversions is described like this in *Great Leaders of the Christian Church*:

> *Both had a momentous experience of evangelical conversion. It lit the fire of evangelistic zeal in their hearts and sent them out, like Whitefield, on a mission to Britain in which they were involved until toward the close of the eighteenth century.*

How perceptive then was the Dean of Westminster, A.P. Stanley, who, in 1876, unveiled a *joint* commemorative tablet to their memory.

While today it is John Wesley who is viewed as the 'Father' of Methodism, it is worth referring to the fact that John saw his brother as a 'co-partner', his frequent expression being 'My brother and I', suggesting strongly how highly he valued Charles's contribution.

What then was Charles's legacy? The starting point must be in terms of his personality. Less combative and autocratic than John, he acted as a restraining influence on his brother, most notably in the relationship between the emerging Methodists and the long-established Church of England. Charles's tact was vitally necessary at a time of great upheaval and even bitterness at the separation.

Charles was also a talented preacher, a wise pastoral counsellor whose gifts and abilities were absolutely dedicated to God. This was something his brother was fully aware of, and highly respected and appreciated.

It is, of course, as a hymn-writer that Charles Wesley is primarily remembered today. His output was vast, and most conservative commentators estimate that he wrote between 6,000 and 7,000 hymns as well as hundreds of poems. For almost fifty years he would write a hymn (or part of one) each and every day. Even on his death-bed he dictated hymns to his followers and family. Inevitably many of his hymns have faded gently away, but the following are still hugely popular, and are sufficient to establish his quality once and for all: 'Christ the Lord is Risen Today', 'Jesu, Lover of

My Soul', 'Hark the Herald Angels Sing', 'Soldiers of Christ Arise', 'O
For a Thousand Tongues to Sing', 'Love Divine All Loves Excelling', 'Lo,
He Comes with Clouds Descending'. One critic has rightly said that he
was a major pioneer in hymn-writing, along with Isaac Watts; until the
eighteenth-century revival, congregational singing was confined to the
rather stilted metrical versions of Scripture. He anticipated the lyrical
poetry outburst early in the next century, and interpreted themes of the
Bible in the language of the heart.

> His hymns ... 'are the possessions of the Christian'.

Sweet singer, sweet song

After his conversion on 21 May 1738, while reading Luther's commentary on
Galatians, Charles Wesley declared: 'I now found myself at peace with God and
rejoiced in hope of loving Christ. I saw that by faith I stood; by the continual support
of faith.' Faith, peace and hope were to be the bulwarks of his life for half a century,
during which time the great doctrines of Christianity found powerful (at times,
sublime) expression in his hymns of praise and worship. His hymns, claims the plaque
on Charles Wesley's house in Bristol, 'are the possessions of the Christian'. No legacy
could be greater or more influential.

Challenge for today

Charles's dedication to hymn-writing was absolute, and he was content for his brother
John to exercise leadership of the Methodist Revival. In this sense, Charles was
secure in the gifts and function God had given him, and so had no wish to trespass
on the work God had called his brother to fulfil. The challenge here is for us to know
God's will for our lives (and ministry) and to get on with it without looking over our
shoulders at other people.

Charles's acceptance of differing roles in ministry stemmed from the peace, faith
and hope that marked his whole life. His example reminds us that we are often
called to different functions in God's kingdom and to accept that fact with grace and

humility. His understanding of God's love in this respect is enshrined in 'Love Divine All Loves Excelling'.

Prayer

Father God, help us to accept the things we cannot change, and to accept the roles You have given us without being jealous of other people. We ask for the grace to fulfil wholeheartedly what You have asked us as individuals to do in Your service. Amen.

JOHN WESLEY
(1703–91)

Evangelist with a burning heart

John Wesley is one of the greatest names in Church history. Like all truly great men, however, he does not fit easily into any category or label. Indeed, Wesley was full of contradictions. To give but two examples, he was the friend of ordinary people yet, at the same time, detested democratic ideals; and he was the deeply loyal son of the Church of England who founded a breakaway denomination (the Methodist Church). A man full of paradoxes he may have been, but there's no doubt whatsoever that his commitment to evangelism and preaching was *absolute*, and from his conversion onwards his evangelism had a number of defined and clear-cut features.

Single-mindedness

With burning zeal and immense spiritual vigour – the like of which is hardly ever seen today – he sought to 'reform the nations, particularly the Church, and to spread Scriptural holiness over the land'. Nothing was allowed to interfere or hinder this. His itinerant ministry took him throughout the United Kingdom many, many times. It is commonly agreed that he travelled at least 250,000 miles in preaching at least 40,000 sermons.

Worldwide vision

Writing to John Harvey, on 25 October 1739, he said:

> But you would have me preach it [the gospel] in a parish. What parish, my brother? I have none at all. Nor I believe ever shall. Must I therefore bury my talent in the earth? Then am I a wicked, unprofitable servant.

In the same year, he declared that he regarded 'the world' as 'his parish'.

Biblically-based

He would certainly echo Paul's words in Galatians 1:12: not a gospel devised by man, but something which came about as a result of a 'revelation from Christ'. In other words, the unchanging, unalterable, transforming gospel of God's power, love and grace. To bring people to an appreciation of 'heart religion' (his phrase), by whatever means, was his overwhelming desire. Truly Wesley was a 'burning heart'. He insisted on the ability of the gospel to transform people, so that the thief stole no more, the drunkard became temperate, the blasphemer became a refined and holy man of God – a message sorely needed in the eighteenth-century, and now. *Sola scriptura, sola fides, sola gratia* were the pillars upon which his sermons were built. And so up and down the country he went with seemingly inexhaustible energy. How was it all possible? Six days before he died, Wesley, writing to William Wilberforce, gives us the answer:

> Unless God has raised you up for this very thing, you will be worn out by the opposition of men and devils; but 'if God be for you, who can be against you?' Are all of them together stronger than God? Oh, 'be not weary in well doing'. Go on, in the name of God and in the power of His might, till even American slavery, the vilest that ever saw the sun, shall vanish away before it.

Post-conversion care

Unlike the Church of England – which was badly, indeed chaotically, disorganised – Methodism from the first was both efficiently and regionally based. Members were placed in Classes (the basic units) of about twelve, which were led by people nominated by Wesley himself; these Classes were part of a Society, groups of which constituted a Circuit, each one being presided over by a Steward. An annual conference was held in London where Wesley gave out orders for the year ahead. Also every Society could have a minister, who received £12 per annum for himself, while a similar sum was paid to his wife, £6 for a servant, and £4 for a child.

... his commitment to evangelism and preaching was absolute ...

Letters

His letters were written amidst a frantically busy and exhausting life. He wrote them without consciously aiming for literary effect. He would often answer as many as thirty letters in a day. On 23 June 1783, for example, he records that his letters that day had cost him eighteen shillings (90p), a sum which, of course, needs to be multiplied scores of times to represent today's value. The letters give a fascinating insight into John Wesley's character and temperament. His passionate nature demonstrated itself time after time in them, particularly with respect to his family, and he was always prepared to deal with their problems. A warm-hearted man, he was often difficult and autocratic (he was not dubbed 'Pope John' without good cause), and yet someone who exercised considerable patience with his somewhat irascible wife. Wesley's letters have been described, perfectly accurately , as the 'marching orders' of the Evangelical Revival, for in them we feel the nerve centre, the throbbing soul of the Methodist awakening. Wesley's letters were, in reality, an extension of his evangelism and pastoral care.

A mirror

John Wesley's letters are significant for another reason too. They are a *mirror* of the Evangelical Revival in the eighteenth century, showing quite clearly how Wesley and his fellow-preachers were called and equipped for service, and how, by following what they felt was God's strategy, they were instrumental in elevating men and women, boys and girls to heights of personal excellence, moral integrity and sublime faith. They also show the change in people's attitude to Wesley until his triumphant death on 2 March 1791; God had indeed been with him, incomparably the best thing of all. Garth Lean, in *John Wesley, Anglican*, says this:

> Wesley's secret was that he sought and found God's fresh ways of bringing
> reality to his generation. He did not pretend that nothing new was needed,
> nor did he water down Christ's commands into a 'new morality' in an attempt
> to titivate the intellectuals or to court the young. He found reality for himself –
> and gave up ease, friends and cherished opinions to take it to the whole nation.

Enshrined here is the secret of John Wesley's towering influence.

Challenge for today

John Wesley's conversion on 24 May 1738, when his heart was 'strangely warmed' by the truth of the gospel, is probably one of the greatest conversions in the history of Christianity. An equally important point is that he continued to be 'strangely warmed' to the end of his life by Jesus' sacrifice on the cross. Do we feel like this? If not, why not? We can rediscover our passion.

Wesley's life stands out as a beacon not just of faith, but also of stick-ability and endurance. Truly for John Wesley, being a Christian was to be engaged in a battle, a 'fight of faith', in which the final outcome – victory – was certain. What an 'overcomer' he was.

Prayer

Heavenly Father, we thank You for the supreme gift of Your Son Jesus. Enable us today, as Wesley did so long ago, to give Him our adoration and praise until we see Him face to face. What a prospect is ahead of us as Christians! Amen.

SUSANNA WESLEY
(1669–1742)

Incredibly capable

S usanna Wesley was a remarkable woman. The youngest of
twenty-five children, her father was Dr Annesley who was
invariably referred to as the 'St Paul of Nonconformity'. In an age
when formal education was not a privilege enjoyed by women, she
taught herself Greek, Hebrew and Latin in order to study the Bible
effectively. Later she married the Reverend Samuel Wesley, a prolific
poet and Anglican clergyman, and gave birth to nineteen children,
though only ten survived to reach adulthood. Life in the Epworth
Rectory was arduous for other reasons too, including her husband's
deep unpopularity with some of his parishioners, poverty, and the
destruction of the old parsonage (by fire) in February 1709.

Mother and educator

Susanna Wesley was, in the historian Stanley Ayling's opinion, a
woman of 'formidable capability' who took pride in the rigorous
efficiency and godliness with which she brought up her children.

Writing to John Wesley about the period after the fire of 1709, she outlined her principles as a parent in terms that must appear forbidding to a modern audience today:

> When the house was rebuilt, and the children all brought home, we entered on a strict reform; and then was begun the custom of singing psalms at beginning and leaving school, morning and evening. Then also that of a general retirement at five o'clock was entered upon, when the oldest took the youngest that could speak, and the second the next, to whom they read the psalms for the day, and a chapter in the New Testament – as in the morning they were directed to read the psalms and a chapter in the Old; after which they went to their private prayers, before they got their breakfast …

This quotation distils the essence of what Susanna called 'a regular method of living' and which later, under the firm guidance of her fifteenth child, John Wesley, characterised the Methodist Church which he founded in 1791.

Parenting

Modern writers have also drawn attention to two other aspects of Susanna Wesley's approach to parenting. First, she regarded parental responsibility as a divine mandate. Second, as Susan Hyatt has so perceptively shown (*Where Are My Susannas?* published in 1997 by Hyatt Intl. Ministries), she believed that *all* talents were God-given and made every effort to discern particular aptitudes for music, rhythm and the balance of words in all her children. Hardly a surprise, then, that one of her children, Charles Wesley, became the hymn-writer par excellence of the eighteenth-century Awakening.

Woman of prayer

Clearly Susanna Wesley was a remarkable person, but what gave her life its evident sense of direction and purpose may be attributed to several other factors. There was, firstly, her deeply devoted prayer life. She took prayer seriously, not only with her children, but in all areas of her life. Out of her daily relationship with God, she was able to nurture what has been called 'The sanctity of the inner conscience'; she was able to support her husband, bring up a large family, and provide a role model – in terms of leadership skills and pastoral guidance – for the women of the Methodist Church. Then, secondly, there was her obedience to the promptings of the Holy Spirit which was, in Hyatt's words, 'grounded in Biblical literacy, theological reflection and personal experience'. This led, in turn, to an absolute dependence on God that did not require either human recognition or approval.

Historical significance

If John Wesley, with considerable justification, is regarded as the 'Father' of Methodism, then Susanna Wesley, with equal justification, must be viewed as its 'Founder'. The reasons for this claim are put cogently by Susan Hyatt in the following way:

> Her perceptive, conscientious guidance during her son's formative years equipped him with biblical tools, theological perspectives, and a holy lifestyle that enabled him to turn a nation from sin to salvation, from near-revolution to rest, from fragmentation to focus, and from instability to solidarity.

... she believed that *all* talents were God-given ...

High praise indeed.

Challenge for today

To many, Susanna Wesley would be seen as impossibly old-fashioned and austere, but two of her main emphases regarding parenting are worth mentioning here:

1. Parenting is a God-given responsibility.
2. All talents are God-given also.

Thus she treated her children as individuals to be nurtured and directed with love and respect.

In addition to bringing up her nineteen children, a Herculean task in itself, Susanna Wesley's leadership skills and positive pastoral guidance made her a role model for women in the Methodist Revival. She illustrates one of the abiding themes of revival: women are to be given an honoured place, not just the men.

Prayer

Heavenly Father, help us to bring up our children in godly ways – and if they are now adults, give us insights on how to advise them in today's often complex world. Amen.

GEORGE WHITEFIELD
(1714–70)

Servant of all

George Whitefield was a titan in an age of titans. Jonathan Edwards, Howell Harris, Daniel Rowland, Charles Wesley and John Wesley all had substantial and lasting achievements to their names, but Whitefield merits equal consideration and respect, even when judged in the light of their majestic qualities and natural aptitudes.

Gloucester and Oxford

Born at The Bell Inn, Gloucester, on 16 December 1714, he was educated at Pembroke College, Oxford. He was an important member of the much derided 'Holy Club', which met in John Wesley's rooms in Lincoln College in the early 1730s, and which later became the model for the classes and societies of the Methodist Revival.

Paradoxically, most of this famous group were converted *after* their days of holy living and good works in Oxford, the first of them being George Whitefield.

Conversion

To understand his later dynamic preaching career, his story has to be retraced to March–April 1735. After a period of intense striving and reading through Joseph Hall's book *Contemplations on the New Testament*, the significance of Jesus' death on the cross became a reality to him and, in John Pollock's words, he realised that

> Man's puny efforts to redeem himself, whether by praying in a storm in Christ Church Walk or schooling his passions or dispensing charity, were incapable of doing what Jesus had already done.

No longer did Whitefield think that forgiveness could be earned or merited, and he was overcome by the glorious simplicity of God's plan of salvation and redemption, the attendant emotion being one of indescribable joy.

That same year (1735), Howell Harris and Daniel Rowland were converted in Wales, followed in 1738 by the conversions of Charles and John Wesley.

1736–70

Ordained in 1736, Whitefield's whole life from that point onwards can be summed up in one word – *preaching*. It is estimated that he preached well over 30,000 sermons in thirty-four years, at least a thousand of them on the text 'Ye must be born again'.

The preaching of the gospel consumed him totally. He felt a divine impulsion to reach as many people as he could each and every day of his life. It was not at all unusual for him to preach five or six times a day, frequently travelling up to sixteen hours in order to make this possible. He often preached the day's first sermon at 5.00am.

Open air preaching

Whitefield was the first member of the 'Holy Club' to preach in the open air. His first congregation was a group of unruly and potentially violent miners, but very soon he was preaching to thousands of men and women at a time. He experienced great difficulty in persuading John and Charles Wesley to follow his example – though later, of course, they did so with conspicuous success. Early in 1739, Whitefield's fiery eloquence had a substantial effect in Bristol and Bath. Stanley Ayling in his biography of John Wesley comments on Whitefield as follows:

> *A natural crowd-compeller, all vehemence and passion and fervour, sentimental to a fault, a master of gesture and histrionics, he was sometimes so moved by his own oratory that it was in danger of being drowned in his own tears.*

Hardly surprisingly, Whitefield exerted an enormous influence wherever he went in England, Scotland, and particularly in America where the effect of his preaching and personal example was quite simply overwhelming. Altogether he visited America seven times, crossing the Atlantic thirteen times in the process.

> Whitefield delighted in the fact that he was a servant of Jesus ...

Perspectives

George Whitefield was a remarkable man, a 'phenomenon', in the opinion of Dr Martyn Lloyd-Jones. He was a

- *Great preacher.* Indeed, there are some who would describe him as the greatest evangelical preacher since the apostle Paul. A more considered view might link his name with that of Hugh Latimer (c.1485–1555) in terms of vivid, forceful and effective preaching.
- *Philanthropist.* He built an orphan house in Georgia, America, and supported it himself throughout his life.
- *Revivalist.* Together with Wesley and Edwards, he was instrumental in leading the great evangelical revivals on both sides of the Atlantic, with all that this meant for the Church and society in the eighteenth century.
- *Servant of all.* This is his own description of himself. He was prepared to help

any evangelical cause without regard for denominational affiliation. In this sense, the only thing that mattered to him was the approval of Jesus Christ. An extract from his Journal shows this unequivocally: 'It is a small thing with us to be judged with the judgement of men – to our own Master we stand or fall.'

He also had an

- *Exhausting lifestyle*. Whitefield's routine was hectic. Rising at 4.00am, he spent an hour in prayer and reading the Bible before starting to preach at 5.00am. Between then and 10.00pm, he occupied himself in letter-writing, travelling, counselling and yet more preaching. Inevitably such a gruelling schedule took its toll physically and mentally and he died at a comparatively young age, on 30 September 1770, in America.

Challenge for today

It is not an exaggeration to claim that Whitefield is one of the giants of revival history, in an age of other giants such as the Wesley brothers and Jonathan Edwards. His influence during his lifetime was extensive, and his example continues to inspire and motivate all those Christians who have an interest in revival.

Whitefield delighted in the fact that he was a servant of Jesus, considering that no greater dignity was possible. He was a remarkable preacher, infusing his sermons with an emotion that his hearers found captivating. One of his most influential sermons was on the text 'You must be born again', and on being asked why he felt this was so vitally important he replied quite simply, 'Because you must be born again.' He would surely endorse the words of the great hymn, 'When I Survey the Wondrous Cross'.

Prayer

Heavenly Father, thank You so much for Your grace and love shown so wonderfully in the gospel. As we contemplate what Jesus did on the cross, our hearts are warmed and invigorated, but please guard them so that they do not become cold and apathetic. Amen.

SMITH WIGGLESWORTH
(1859–1947)

Apostle of faith

Smith Wigglesworth died in 1947 aged eighty-seven. His life
therefore predated the charismatic movement which was later
to invigorate the life of the Church worldwide. Yet his name is
constantly invoked in articles and books dealing with the charismatic
phenomenon as an example of someone who operated powerfully in
the gifts of the Spirit. By any reckoning, Smith Wigglesworth was
a remarkable man who enjoyed robust, even rude, health right up
to and including the day of his death. On 12 March 1947 he merely
closed his eyes and slipped into eternity, thus bringing to a close
a life of unceasing endeavour which had inspired men and women
throughout the world. As a close acquaintance commented, 'To know
Wigglesworth was a never-to-be-forgotten experience. To fellowship
with him left an indelible mark upon the life of those thus privileged.'

Humble origins

If his influence was extensive, his origins were certainly humble and unpretentious. Essentially unschooled and a plumber by trade (in Bradford), he was a simple and ordinary man. Physically he was a 'commanding figure with twinkling small eyes in a stout face, rugged and refined at the same time, always dressed immaculately in a dark suit'. While in purely human terms he would be viewed as entirely unimportant and insignificant, he was spiritually a giant in every sense of this word.

Powerful man of God

What qualities, then, made Smith Wigglesworth such a powerful man of God?

- *He had a high regard for the Word of God.* Quite literally, the only book he read was the Bible. One of his biographers, Albert Hibbert, says, 'Many today might consider this unusual, even quaint behaviour, but to Wigglesworth it was perfectly normal. It is tempting to add that the Word of God was the source of his strength.'
- *He was a man of prayer.* He said himself that he never spent more than half an hour at a time praying, but that he never went half an hour without praying. This was the secret of his power as an evangelist, preacher and man of God.
- *His obedience to the Holy Spirit.* In one of his most famous sermons, Wigglesworth declared:

I see everything a failure except that which is done in the Spirit. But as you live in the Spirit, you move, act, eat, drink, and do everything to the glory of God. Our message is always this: 'Be filled with the Spirit'. This is God's place for you, and it is as far above the natural life as the heavens are above the earth. Yield yourselves for God to fill. ('Life in the Spirit', published in Ever Increasing Faith*).*

- *He was a man of faith.* As long ago as 1924, Wigglesworth exhorted his hearers:

These are days when we need to have our faith strengthened, when we need to know God who has declared that the just shall live by faith. Any man can be changed by faith, no matter how he may be fettered. Man cannot live by bread alone, but must live by every word that proceedeth out of the mouth of God. This is the food of faith.

The combination outlined above is as significant today as it was for Smith Wigglesworth: from the bedrock of the reality of the Word of God, he prayed unceasingly, with faith, and under the guidance and motivation of the Holy Spirit. He moved with a simplicity, joy and confidence, a frequent note in his sermons being this unshakeable assurance:

We have a big God. We have a wonderful Jesus. We have a glorious Comforter. God's canopy is over you and will cover you at all times, preserving you from evil. Under His wings shall thou trust. The Word of God is living and powerful and in its treasures you will find eternal life. If you dare trust this wonderful Lord, this Lord of life, you will find in Him everything you need. You will find that if you dare trust Him, He will never fail.

All that mattered … was listening for and to the voice of God's Holy Spirit …

This was precisely the sort of robustness that made Wigglesworth one of the great spiritual leaders in the first half of the twentieth century. Nor is it any surprise that supernatural events attended his meetings.

Miraculous healings

Wigglesworth was wonderfully used by God in the healing ministry, which he viewed not as something in addition to his preaching of the Word of God, but integral to it. Many instances could be cited, but the case of a five-year-old boy who had died is worth recalling. He was laid out in the family home for friends and acquaintances to pay their last respects. Such a poignant sight moved Wigglesworth to tears and, after locking the door behind the family mourners, 'He lifted the still form of the lad from the coffin and stood it up in the corner of the room. He rebuked death in the name of the Lord Jesus, and commanded it to surrender its victim: the child returned to life' (quoted in *Smith Wigglesworth: The Secret of His Power*, p.45).

Lessons of life and ministry

Over sixty years have elapsed since Wigglesworth's death, during which time the charismatic movement has refreshed and motivated the Church globally, and imbued it with a clearer awareness of worship and the conception of the Fatherhood of God. What are the lessons of his life and ministry for today? The starting point must be that God does not want us to imitate Wigglesworth slavishly so as to produce the signs and wonders that attended his services. Rather, God wants us to be ourselves, but to realise and act upon the understanding of what *we* can be in God, effectively serving Him where we are, and with the gifts we possess.

All that mattered to Wigglesworth was listening for and to the voice of God's Holy Spirit: it is hardly any wonder his ministry had such a powerful anointing.

Challenge for today

Stories about Wigglesworth are legion, even six decades after his death, such was the force of his ministry, personality and faith. The temptation for us today is to attempt to replicate Wigglesworth's way of ministering. Instead, we must forge our own ways of ministering, as led and guided by the Holy Spirit. The secret of Wigglesworth's life was unremitting prayer. He conceived of revival in typically robust terms: that it can only come when we are prepared to die to self and human striving. Alongside this insistence was his teaching that Jesus must occupy the foremost place in our hearts and lives.

Prayer

Father God, enlarge our thinking so that we are men and women of God in a true sense, full of faith and expectancy. Help us to be obedient to Your calling, whatever the cost. Amen.

DAVID YONGGI CHO
(born 1936)

Man of faith

Dr David (formerly Paul) Yonggi Cho is senior pastor of Yoide Full Gospel Central Church, Seoul, South Korea. With a congregation of over 750,000, it is easily the world's largest church. Its growth from a membership of 600 in 1961 (through 11,000 in 1973) has been truly phenomenal, though Cho himself takes no credit for it. Self-effacingly, he says, 'No revival should be the product of a single personality', adding, 'I do not claim to be responsible for the revival that is occurring in our church. In fact, the revival continues whether I am there or not.' His attitude in this sense is much the same as that of Evan Roberts during the Welsh Revival of 1904–05, attributing the dynamic revival solely to the sovereign activity of God. This startling growth could hardly have been foreseen when, aged nineteen, Cho, a devotee of Buddhism, was not only struggling desperately to survive financially, but was also diagnosed as having incurable tuberculosis, with a maximum life expectancy of three to four months. Death seemed imminent.

Dramatic conversion

God, however, had other ideas. Cho records what happened next in his preface to *The Fourth Dimension*, a manual for church growth and renewal. Exhorted, a few days after receiving his grim medical prognosis, by a young female high school student to 'Search the Bible … if you read it faithfully you will find the words of life', he was, at first, repelled by the apparent 'foolishness' of the Book. He did though find one striking theme: Jesus Christ the Son of God. The close proximity of his own death convinced him that he needed someone greater than a religion or a philosophy – certainly something more dynamic than mere sympathy to cope with the ills and complexities of human existence. That Someone he discovered to be Jesus Christ. He said: 'Convinced that Jesus Christ was alive and moved by the vitality of His ministry, I knelt down and I asked Christ to come into my heart, to save, heal and deliver me from death.'

Changed direction

Cho never found out who the young girl was, but leaving the sterility of Buddhism behind him, he trained for the Christian ministry at an Assemblies of God Bible school and, in 1958, he started his first church in an old American service tent situated next to a rubbish dump. Hardly a promising situation, but within twenty years it had become the largest church in the world.

Recipe for success

Why has God used David Yonggi Cho in such remarkable ways? Two reasons spring immediately to mind: his *humility* and his *obedience*. He frequently asserts, 'It is not me but God working through me', adding: 'I pray and I obey.' There is also his unyielding faith. 'God,' he says, 'is not going to do anything for you without coming through your own life. God will never bring about any of His great works without coming through your own personal faith.' Then, there is prayer. It is the highest priority of Cho's life. He spends several hours each (and every) day in prayer and expects his assistant pastors to pray at least three hours daily.

Symbolising this fervent commitment – both personally and collectively – is the International Prayer Mountain with its round-the-clock day and night praying. Colin Whittaker, in *Prayer Mountains*, described the experience at Prayer Mountain as

> Being engulfed in wave after wave of praying voices, which rise and fall only to rise again with even greater noise and fervency. To gaze around brings no relief for you find yourself surrounded by a forest of hands, a fervent physical expression of the intense intercession in which they are engaging. It is both frightening and challenging.

It is particularly so when 'they pray for the salvation of lost souls: they really believe people will be lost for ever unless they receive the Gospel of Christ.'

Prayer is the key

For David Yonggi Cho, prayer is the key: for the life of faith and holiness, for evangelism, for church growth and for the coming of revival. Dr Martyn Lloyd-Jones once wrote: 'Prayer is the ultimate test of a man's true spiritual condition. There is nothing that tells the truth about us as Christian people so much as our prayer life.' Viewed in this light, Dr David Yonggi Cho and his church are prayer partners extraordinary.

'No revival should be the product of a single personality' ...

Challenge for today

Though leader of probably the largest church in the world, he is insistent that the *only hero* in the Church is the Lord Jesus, a corrective much needed in the publicity-consciousness Christian world today.

Yonggi Cho is equally insistent that the growth of his church is due to God's sovereign activity – another lesson all Christians need to learn. To these perceptions must be added his total commitment to prayer.

129

Prayer

Father God, You are the supreme One in the universe You have created. Please enable us to put this truth into practice in our lives each day. Give us also the humility to learn from other Christians. Amen.

SOME REFLECTIONS: THE GOLDEN THREADS

Dependence on God, albeit in different ways and in different circumstances, characterised the lives of these men and women we have described. They were significant, in some cases globally, and had an abiding influence, not because of their own strength, abilities and aptitudes, but because of their humble reliance on God for their sustenance and equipping. In other words, God made them great. That was the secret of their effectiveness, and it is a principle that holds good today in a world that celebrates preening self-confidence, assertiveness and often grotesque individualism aptly summed up by the song, 'I Did It My Way'. In contrast, the people we have read about knew where to go for their 'refuge and strength' (Psa. 46:1), nurturing their spiritual lives in the 'secret place' of prayer and restful confidence in God (Psa. 91, AV).

For many of them, too, reading about previous revivals was a tonic, refreshment and an encouragement. Two such men were Robert Murray McCheyne and Evan Roberts who famously said, 'I could sit up all night to talk and read about revivals.' Their enthusiasm should not cause any surprise because in revivals there is an effusion of the Holy Spirit and a return to the events of Pentecost. Luke's thrilling account of that tumultuous day preserves the following features: excitement, a dynamic sense of God's presence, powerful preaching of the gospel, converted and changed consciences, events of supernatural power attendant on the disciplined, accurate, precise and obedient preaching of God's Word, and an emphatic focus on the Person and work of the Lord Jesus.

The people referred to in this book were also notable for six golden threads that marked out their lives:

1. Submission to the teaching of the Bible.
2. Openness to the supernatural guidance of the Holy Spirit.
3. Deep devotion to prayer and worship.
4. Integrity of lifestyle in terms of transformed behaviour.
5. An intense desire to glorify Jesus.
6. Humility.

These men and women did not pursue revival phenomena (or revivalism) as the latest fad or gimmick, thereby hoping to gain some publicity for their church or their ministries. They pursued the Lord Jesus desiring, as with the apostle Paul, 'to know [him] and the power of his resurrection' (Phil. 3:10) in their daily lives. Holiness, restoration and forgiveness were at the centre of everything they did. With such people, signs and wonders accompanied and confirmed the preaching of the gospel to those who were not Christians (Heb. 2:1–4), eloquently demonstrating a return to apostolic Christianity in all its pristine beauty and power.

So, to summarise: these people, often in the bleakest of circumstances, pursued God, His presence and cleansing power with a determined realism that we would do well to emulate today. What a challenge and motivation for all God's people in the twenty-first century.

CONCLUSION

And finally ... we must go on.

'God's recipe for revival has at its heart a radical and demanding re-engagement with the word of the gospel that will reorder the whole life of the church.' (Tom Smail)

'Revival is not the church filled with people; it is the church filled with God.' (Duncan Campbell)

In a perceptive article entitled 'God in top gear: the reality of revival', the Reverend Tom Smail quotes a conversation that occurred over fifty years ago. A professor of theology, at the end of a game of golf, was told that what his church needed was revival. 'Yes, indeed,' he replied, 'but the question is, what kind of revival?' His golfing companion's immediate reply, 'As far as I am concerned, *any kind of revival of revival*' probably encapsulates the feelings and yearnings of vast numbers of contemporary Christians across the world. (Quoted in an article in *Quiet Spaces*, published in Abingdon by The Bible Reading Fellowship, 2007.)

Such a longing is inextricably linked to the abject state of the Church in many countries, especially in the Western world. It also has its genesis in an awareness of God's powerful interventions in the past in reviving His people: the dead bones can live again.

Is revival, however, the *only answer* to the current malaise within the Church? This may not be a popular or comfortable question with those who have read about, waited and prayed for revival in a consistent and dedicated manner, but it must be faced honestly and realistically. This is what Cleland Thom did in his book *Broken-Hearted Believers*. He made this courageous statement:

> Britain will, I believe, only see revival after the church has been broken of its adolescent strength by a period of testing, tears and persecution. At the moment, we are in our teens: strong, enthusiastic, full of youthful arrogance and ready to take on the world and the devil, and maybe even the flesh. But perhaps we are forgetting that God only uses broken vessels.

Tentatively it is suggested that a balanced response to the question 'Is revival the only answer?' would involve an understanding of three things. First, a clear understanding of the true nature of revival: an unusual, independent, mighty and sovereign act of God that is totally beyond human initiatives (however worthy or energetic or prayerful) to achieve. Second, an equally clear awareness of the effect of such a divine intervention. Revival awakens the Church to its true function, which is to be His holy presence and power in the world, and to influence all denominations, leading to a joyous spiritual unity (see Psa. 133) among Christians. Third, it causes Christians to commit themselves to a particular lifestyle characterised by humility, prayer, an acute awareness of sin and pride, and a willingness to seek God seriously (see 2 Chron. 7:14).

These are precisely the qualities that characterise the people featured in the biographies that form the major part of this publication. In good times and bad, in times of blessing and dryness, in times of success and failure they stuck tenaciously to the vision that was God-given, placed their trust and confidence in Him alone, and balanced God's sovereignty against human responsibility. This principle is made absolutely clear in Philippians 2:12–13: 'Therefore, my dear friends … work out your salvation with fear and trembling, for it is God who works in you to will and to act according to his good purpose.' It is vitally important to observe the context of these verses, which follow the great hymn extolling Jesus as God's humble servant; we too are to serve God – in revival times or not – in the same spirit, by the power of His (Jesus') Spirit. We are to

- pray that we might be continually filled with the Spirit (Eph. 5:18);
- take care not to grieve the Holy Spirit (Eph. 4:30);
- pray and expect that the Holy Spirit will convict the world (John 16:8–11).

Now we come to perhaps the most difficult and, in many senses, the most agonising question of all: what are we to do if revival does not come? In this context, further reference may be made to Cleland Thom's robust and iconoclastic book, *Broken-Hearted Believers*. He makes the astute observation that many Christians, not just in Britain but also across the world, have been praying and waiting for revival so long that they have become weary, discouraged, even disillusioned. 'Hope deferred makes the heart sick' (Prov. 13:12). In this sense, rash promises (however august or famous the persons making them) are to be avoided at all costs, Thom suggests – a corrective I most certainly acquiesce to, because it casts deep suspicions on the prophetic ministry.

In private conversation, the late Dr Martyn Lloyd-Jones was asked what we should do if revival does not come. His reply, at once immediate and crisp, was: 'We go on.' But doing what? In the light of the biographies of the revivalists in this book, it is to:

Desire God's presence. In the 1904–05 Welsh Revival, the presence of the Lord was so strong that no one could imagine uttering expletives or performing ungodly acts. And those who were present 'could only describe His presence as being absolutely beyond description. The promptings of the Holy Spirit were so distinct that thousands would simultaneously spring to their feet in worship in such perfect unison that those who witnessed it considered it miraculous' (Rick Joyner). On such occasions the glory of God was the pre-eminent longing on the part of the worshippers.

Be obedient to God's Word. It is the knowledge of the will of God through the teaching of His Word that imparts confidence in asking God for revival. This is infinitely more important than possessing knowledge about Jonathan Edwards, Martin Luther or Smith Wigglesworth. Revival is quite simply the Holy Spirit refreshing the Church with His revelation and equipping men and women to enter into a deeper relationship with Him. Selwyn Hughes captures something of this dynamic when he says that 'Revival is God pushing [people] toward repentance, holiness and the cleansing of our souls. The powerful wind of the Spirit removes corrosion from our souls and cleanses the heart.'

Pray without ceasing. Prayer is an absolute priority both before and during revivals. Although Spurgeon's prayers, as noted in the chapter on him, were not normally recorded, the following is his prayer for revival:

> *O God, send us the Holy Ghost. Give us both the breath of spiritual life and the fire of unconquerable zeal. O Thou art our God, answer us by fire, we pray Thee. Answer us both by wind and fire, and then we shall see Thee to be God indeed. The kingdom comes not, and the work is flagging. Oh that Thou*

wouldst send the wind and the fire. Thou wilt do this when we are all of one accord, all believing, all expecting, all prepared for revival. Lord bring us to this waiting state. God send us a season of glorious disorder. Oh for a sweep of the wind that will set the seas in motion, and make our ironclad brethren lying so quietly at anchor to roll from stem to stern. Break down every barrier that hinders the incoming of Thy might. Give us now both hearts of flame and tongues of fire to preach Thy reconciling Word, for Jesus' sake. Amen.

It was similarly dynamic praying that led to the 1859–60 Revival in Britain and abroad. It not only led to the revival but also sustained and spread it. Prayer meetings took place at all hours of the day and night; weekly prayer meetings became daily ones and increased in numbers. Christians from different denominations joined together, many of the meetings taking place on premises other than churches. There is a challenge implicit in these facts: do we pray with Christians other than those from our own church? Sadly for most of us the answer to this question would be a resounding negative.

Revival does not, however, come cheaply. This is made clear in one of Duncan Campbell's sermons, in which he identifies four cardinal principles:

1. The sovereignty of God. By this, Campbell meant allowing God to have His way in the lives of men and women.
2. True hunger for God. The promise remains as valid today as when it was first written that those who 'hunger and thirst for righteousness … will be filled' (Matt. 5:6).
3. Getting right with God. Campbell is direct and unequivocal: 'If you want revival get right with God. If you are not prepared to do this, stop talking about revival, your talking and praying is but the laughing-stock of devils.'
4. Intercessory prayer. Seeking God with clean hands and a pure heart (Psa. 24:3–4) leads to an awareness of God's glory, in response to which He can move in supernatural power and flood the barren places with what Campbell memorably calls the 'reviving balm of the Holy Spirit'. (Summarised from *The Price And Power of Revival* (London: Scripture Illustrations Ltd, 1956).

In the dark days of the Second World War, Dr Martyn Lloyd-Jones wrote to a fellow minister, saying:

> *The only hope, I see more and more, is a Revival. I feel we are all called to pray and to prepare for such a movement. Nothing else can possibly deal with the terrible state of the country and of the world. In any case our business is to sow the seed in hope, knowing that God alone can give the increase. Do not allow the devil to discourage you.*

Over sixty years from those unremittingly bleak days, Lloyd-Jones's comments are as pertinent as they were then. Almost four years later, in a letter to the Reverend Philip Hughes, he reiterated similar views, declaring that nothing but an 'unusual and signal manifestation of God's power through the Holy Spirit can possibly meet the present need. I pray daily for revival and try to exhort my people to do the same'. He continued to pray for revival until he died on 1 March 1981.

Knowing about revival is not, however, enough. Being able to define it, analyse it, and discuss it with assurance is not enough, either. Knowing key facts about great revivalists, or knowledgeably discussing the defining moments in revival history is, at best, theoretical. What is required is that Christians, through persistent prayer and openness to the directive guidance of the Holy Spirit, enter into a transforming intimacy with the living God, and are committed to a life of personal holiness and forgiveness. The Spirit is waiting expectantly to touch every part of *your* church, from the exhausted, overworked pastor, to the often dysfunctional leaders, to the cantankerous men and women in the pews – and is eager to show them that they can be filled to overflowing with a power and a presence far in excess of anything they ever thought possible. The Church local and worldwide can once again experience the radical cleaning and empowering of 'God in top gear', but it starts, as it inevitably must, with *you*. Are *you* willing to face the challenge? Only *you* know.

Notes

Quotations from the primary sources, here listed alphabetically, are gratefully acknowledged:

Dr Martyn Lloyd-Jones, *Letters 1919–1981* (Edinburgh: Banner of Truth Trust, 1994).
Rick Joyner, *The World Aflame* (North Carolina: Morning Star Publications, 1993).
Tom Smail, *In Quiet Spaces* (Oxford: The Bible Reading Fellowship, 2007).
Cleland Thom, *Broken-Hearted Believers* (Eastbourne: Kingsway Publications, 1998).

For further information about CWR, its ministry, the life of Selwyn Hughes, and further helpful resources, visit **www.cwr.org.uk**

SELECT BIBLIOGRAPHY

Kevin Adams, *A Diary of Revival* (Farnham: CWR, 2004); and *A Pictorial History of Revival* (Farnham: CWR, 2004).

Dr John H. Armstrong *When God Moves* (Oregon: Harvest House Publications, 1998).

Stanley Ayling, *John Wesley* (London: Collins, 1979).

Robert Backhouse (ed.), *Spurgeon on Revival* (Eastbourne: Kingsway Publications, 1996).

E.G. Carre (ed.), *Praying Hyde* (New Jersey: Bridge Publishing, 1982).

Robert E. Coleman (ed.), *The Heart of John Wesley's Journal* (East Lothian: Labarum Publications, 1979).

Albert W. Edsor, *Set Your Home in Order: God's Call to George Jeffreys* (Chichester: New Wine Press, 1989).

Donald Dayton (compiler), *C.G. Finney: Reflections on Revival* (Minneapolis, Minnesota: Bethany House Publications, 1979).

Jack Deere, *Surprised By The Voice of God* (Eastbourne: Kingsway Publications, 2005).

Dr Lewis Drummond, *Eight Keys to Biblical Revival* (Minneapolis, Minnesota: Bethany House Publications, 1994).

Brian Edwards, *Revival: A People Saturated with God* (Darlington: Evangelical Press, first published 1990).

Norman P. Grubb, *Rees Howells: Intercessor* (London: Lutterworth Press, London, 1952; Second edition 1967).

Albert Hibbert, *Smith Wigglesworth: The Secret of His Power* (Chichester: Sovereign World, 1982).

Selwyn Hughes, *Revival: Times of Refreshing* (Farnham: CWR, first published 1984); and *My Story* (Farnham: CWR, 2004).

Brynmor Pierce Jones, *An Instrument of Revival: The Complete Life of Evan Roberts* (New Jersey: Bridge Publishers, 1995); *The Trials and Triumphs of Jessie Penn-Lewis* (New Jersey: Bridge-Logos Publishers, 1997); and *Voices From the Welsh Revival* (Mid-Glamorgan: Bryntirion Press, 1998).

John Kilpatrick, *Feast of Fire* (London: Marshall Pickering, 1995).

David Long, *Revival: A Study in Biblical Patterns* (Kilmarnock, Scotland: John Ritchie, 1992).

Garth Lean, *John Wesley, Anglican* (London: Blandford Press, 1964).

Dr Martyn Lloyd-Jones, *Preaching and Preachers* (London: Hodder & Stoughton, 1971); *Revival: can we make it happen?* (London: Marshall Pickering, 1986); and *The Puritans: Their Origins and Successors* (Edinburgh, Banner of Truth, 1987).

David Petts, *Just a Taste of Heaven: a biblical and balanced approach to God's healing power* (Mattersey, England: Mattersey Hall, 2006).

John Pollock, *Wilberforce* (Eastbourne: Kingsway Publications, 2007).

Winkie Pratney, *Revival: Principles to Change the World* (Texas: Whitaker House, 1983).

Leonard Ravenhill, *Why Revival Tarries* (Eastbourne: Kingsway Publications, 1998).

Dr Raymond C. Ortlund, *Revival Sent From God* (Leicester: Inter-Varsity Press, 2000).

B.A. Ramsbottom, *Christmas Evans* (Luton: The Bunyan Press, 1985).

Dr Mark Stibbe, *Times of Refreshing: A Practical Theology of Revival For Today* (London: Marshall Pickering, 1985); and *Thinking Clearly About Revival* (Oxford: Monarch Books, 1998).

David Yonggi Cho, *Prayer That Brings Revival* (Florida: Creation House, 1996); and *Fourth Dimension* (Gainesville, FL: Bridge-Logos Publishers, 1979).

Arthur Wallis, *Rain From Heaven: Revival in Scripture and History* (London: Hodder & Stoughton, 1979).

Colin Whittaker, *Great Revivals* (London: Marshall Pickering, 1990); *Prayer Mountains* (London: Marshall Pickering); and *Seven Pentecostal Pioneers* (Basingstoke: Marshall, Morgan & Scott, 1983).

John D. Woodbridge (ed.), *Great Leaders of the Christian Church* (Chicago: Moody Press, 1988).